Construct Game Development
Beginner's Guide

A guide to escalate beginners to intermediate game creators through teaching practical game creation using Scirra Construct

Daven Bigelow

PACKT PUBLISHING

open source
community experience distilled

BIRMINGHAM - MUMBAI

Construct Game Development
Beginner's Guide

First published: May 2012

Production Reference: 1110512

Published by Packt Publishing Ltd.
Livery Place
35 Livery Street
Birmingham B3 2PB, UK.

ISBN 978-1-84951-660-0

www.packtpub.com

Cover Image by Vinayak Chittar (vinayak.chittar@gmail.com)

Credits

Author

Daven Bigelow

Reviewer

D.M. Noyé

Acquisition Editor

Usha Iyer

Lead Technical Editor

Shreerang Deshpande

Technical Editors

Unnati Shah

Mehreen Shaikh

Project Coordinator

Alka Nayak

Proofreader

Jonathan Todd

Indexer

Rekha Nair

Graphics

Manu Joseph

Production Coordinators

Prachali Bhiwandkar

Nilesh R. Mohite

Cover Work

Nilesh R. Mohite

About the Author

Daven Bigelow is a hobby game developer and a software programmer. He has been creating 2D games for over eight years, across different game creation tools and programming languages. However, most of his experience lies in Construct Classic, which has been his tool of choice over the last three years.

He can often be found on the Scirra forums under the name Jayjay, where he provides advice and examples for new users seeking help.

I would like to thank all my friends and family who encouraged me along the way. I also send thanks to the publisher, Packt Publishing, and all of its employees for their efforts.

Lastly, I thank you, the reader, for reading this book. I hope that it meets all of your expectations.

About the Reviewer

D.M. Noyé is a successful entrepreneur with extensive experience working on major commercial projects with a number of large corporations, as well as independent ventures spanning several fields, from music and literary arts to video games.

I'd like to thank the entire Scirra Construct community and development team for all of their years of hard work and dedication and for always being willing to share their insights and talents, making it possible for me to gain knowledge of how to use this great development tool and pass on that knowledge to others.

www.PacktPub.com

Support files, eBooks, discount offers and more

You might want to visit www.PacktPub.com for support files and downloads related to your book.

Did you know that Packt offers eBook versions of every book published, with PDF and ePub files available? You can upgrade to the eBook version at www.PacktPub.com, and as a print book customer, you are entitled to a discount on the eBook copy. Get in touch with us at service@packtpub.com for more details.

At www.PacktPub.com, you can also read a collection of free technical articles, sign up for a range of free newsletters, and receive exclusive discounts and offers on Packt books and eBooks.

http://PacktLib.PacktPub.com

Do you need instant solutions to your IT questions? PacktLib is Packt's online digital book library. Here, you can access, read and search across Packt's entire library of books.

Why Subscribe?

- ◆ Fully searchable across every book published by Packt
- ◆ Copy and paste, print and bookmark content
- ◆ On demand and accessible via web browser

Free Access for Packt account holders

If you have an account with Packt at www.PacktPub.com, you can use this to access PacktLib today and view nine entirely free books. Simply use your login credentials for immediate access.

I dedicate this book to my cousin Ken, who first inspired me to make video games.

Table of Contents

Preface	**1**
Chapter 1: Our First Look at Construct	**5**
The first step: downloading and installing Construct Classic	5
Time for action – getting Construct Classic up and running	6
Step two: creating a game project	7
Time for action – starting a game project	7
Creating the project	10
Changing the project details	10
Running the project	10
Step three: navigating the interface of Construct Classic	11
Time for action – clicking our way around Construct Classic	11
The layout editor	15
The properties box	15
The event editor	15
The animator box	15
The layers box	15
The final step: an introduction to objects	16
Time for action – creating some objects	16
Creating an object	24
Drawing the sprite	24
Changing the appearance of the sprite	27
Summary	27
Chapter 2: Hello World! Construct Style	**29**
Sprites revisited	30
Time for action – creating a player sprite	30
Creating new animations	39
Animation tags	40
Choosing the Collisions mode	40

Tiled backgrounds: defining the world	**40**
Time for action – make some tiled backgrounds	**41**
Attributes: telling Construct more about our objects	**46**
Time for action – adding attributes to our objects	**46**
Behaviors: teaching objects how to act	**49**
Time for action – getting our player moving	**49**
The behaviors	53
Setting controls	53
Variables: private and global	**53**
Time for action – giving our player a life	**54**
Textboxes: giving the player a heads-up	**55**
Time for action – showing our player their health and score	**56**
Events: setting the rules and goals of a game	**59**
Time for action – very eventful games	**60**
The sprites	67
Events	68
Conditions	68
Actions	68
Summary	**68**
Chapter 3: Adding the Challenge	**69**
Before we start	**69**
Reaching the goal	**69**
Time for action – making the game winnable	**70**
Overlapping versus collision	72
Set activated	72
Set animation	72
Avoid the hazards	**72**
Time for action – bestowing more challenges on a player	**73**
The death of a player	77
Resurrecting our player	77
Giving the player a game over	77
Putting some bad guys in	**77**
Time for action – adding an enemy and making him move	**78**
Direction of motion	84
Falling down	84
Turning around	84
Looking for a hit	84
Improving our interface	**84**
Time for action – creating a background for the GUI	**85**
Summary	**89**

Chapter 4: Making Noise   91
A game and its music   91
Time for action – add some music to our game   92
   The start of layout condition   94
   Playing the music file   94
   Looping the music file   94
Modules of music   94
Time for action – play some mod music   95
   The Is playing condition   99
   Loading and playing the file   99
Sounds: describing the action   99
Time for action – adding sounds   99
Exporting our game   104
Time for action – exporting our game   104
A note on sharing our games   110
Summary   111

Chapter 5: Practical Physics   113
Creating physical objects   114
Time for action – creating our objects   114
   The Global property   127
   Aligning to a grid   128
   Setting the Physics properties   128
   The Timer behavior   128
   Creating a custom physics collision mask   128
Event sheets and groups   128
Time for action – creating and using Event sheets and groups 129
Adding a physical force   130
Time for action – creating forces   131
Adding special pegs   136
Time for action – creating specialty pegs   136
   The For loop   142
   Set timescale   142
Portals: a way of getting from A to B   142
Time for action – teleporting the ball   142
Particle objects: creating a fireworks finale   143
Time for action – creating fireworks   144
Playing the sounds and music   148
Time for action – adding the sounds and music   148
Creating another level   152
Time for action – making another level   152

Meet the debugger	**154**
Time for action – looking through the debugger	**154**
Summary	**156**
Chapter 6: Custom Levels	**157**
The user friendly INI file	**157**
Time for action – creating an INI file	**158**
INI groups	160
INI items	160
Loading levels	**160**
Time for action – load custom levels	**160**
Setting the INI file	165
Loading the level	165
Including the Game event sheet	165
The NextINI layout	165
The Game Over screen	**165**
Time for action – creating the Game Over layout	**166**
Making a level editor	**170**
Time for action – creating the objects	**171**
Time for action – loading and saving levels with events	**174**
Time for action – creating events for the interface	**181**
The edit region	188
The function object	188
Enabling and disabling groups	188
Writing to an INI file	188
Positioning the Cursor object to a grid	189
Placing portals	189
Summary	**190**
Chapter 7: Platformer Revisited, a 2D Shooter	**191**
Before we start	**191**
Multiplayer: getting your friends involved	**192**
Time for action – creating the game assets and title screen	**192**
Time for action – designing the level	**195**
Time for action – creating player characters and conveyor belt objects	**197**
Time for action – creating the HUD objects	**205**
Time for action – creating the main game events	**207**
Time for action – creating the Game Over layout	**217**
Families	218
Containers	218
Multiplayer	219
Static scrolling	219

Shooting bullets	**219**
Time for action – adding some guns	**219**
Parallax: giving the impression of depth	**227**
Time for action – creating parallax scrolling	**228**
Lights and shadows: illuminating the darkness	**229**
Time for action – using lights and shadow casters	**230**
Enemies with guns: slightly more challenging	**232**
Time for action – making some enemies	**232**
Manual collision detection	238
Basic AI	238
Spawning a gun	238
Summary	**239**
Chapter 8: I'm Throwing a Grenade!	**241**
Grenades – bouncing, timed explosives	**241**
Time for action – throwing grenades	**242**
Throwing the grenade	246
Bouncing the grenades	246
Explosions – big bright lights	**246**
Time for action – explosion flashes	**247**
Effects – distortions and other nice things	**249**
Time for action – adding some distortion	**249**
Pixel shaders	251
The effects used	252
Objects – completely blown away	**252**
Time for action – blast the robots away	**252**
Summary	**254**
Chapter 9: Our Final Moments	**255**
What we've learned	**255**
Chapter 1, the basics of the Construct Classic editor	255
Chapter 2, our first game, MyPlatformer	256
Chapter 3, adding enemies and a lives system	256
Chapter 4, playing sounds and music	256
Chapter 5, a physics game	256
Chapter 6, custom levels and level editors	256
Chapter 7, A sidescrolling shooter	257
Chapter 8, effects and physics interactions	257
Extending our games	**257**
MyPlatformer	257
BounceBall	258
SideShooter	258

Tips and tricks — 258
  Custom collision masks — 258
  Adding custom plugins — 262
  Adding custom effects — 262
  Using the Canvas object — 262
  Using the Minimap object — 263
  Using the Plasma object — 264
  Make backups often; make saves even more — 265
  Finding help — 266
A note on Construct 2 — 266
Summary — 267
Appendix: Pop Quiz Answers — 269
  Chapter 3: Adding the Challenge — 269
    Recap — 269
  Chapter 4: Making Noise — 269
    Sound and music — 269
  Chapter 5: Practical Physics — 270
    Physical games — 270
  Chapter 6: Custom Levels — 270
    INI file recap — 270
  Chapter 7: Platformer Revisited, a 2D Shooter — 271
    A shot in the dark — 271
  Chapter 8: I'm Throwing a Grenade! — 271
    Looking back on timers and effects — 271
Index — 273

Preface

Welcome to *Construct Game Development Beginner's Guide*. In this book, you will be learning to use the free and open source software Construct Classic to make your own video games from scratch.

Construct Classic is a DirectX 9-based game creation environment for Windows, designed for making 2D games. Construct Classic uses a graphical event-based system for defining how the game behaves, in a visual, human-readable way—you do not need to program or script anything at all. It's intuitive for beginners, but powerful enough for advanced users to work without hindrance.

So, if you have ever wanted to make video games, and haven't tried before, this book will help you get started!

What this book covers

Chapter 1, Our First Look at Construct, covers the basics of the Construct Classic editor.

Chapter 2, Hello World! Construct Style, covers the making our first game, a classic platformer.

Chapter 3, Adding the Challenge, covers creating enemies and a goal for our platform game.

Chapter 4, Making Noise, covers playing music and sound files in Construct Classic.

Chapter 5, Practical Physics, covers making our second game with the built-in physics engine.

Chapter 6, Custom Levels, covers making a level editor to save and load external level files.

Chapter 7, Platformer Revisited, a 2D Shooter, covers learning to make a platform shooter.

Chapter 8, I'm Throwing a Grenade, involves learning to use pixel shader effects in our games.

Chapter 9, Our Final Moments, covers a summary of what we've learned and some extra tips.

What you need for this book

With screenshots and step-by-step instructions, this beginner's guide requires only an interest in making video games, and basic experience with the Windows operating system.

Who this book is for

If you have ever thought of making a 2D computer game of your own, this book is for you.

Conventions

In this book, you will find several headings appearing frequently.

To give clear instructions of how to complete a procedure or task, we use:

Time for action – heading

1. Action 1

2. Action 2

3. Action 3

Instructions often need some extra explanation so that they make sense, so they are followed with:

What just happened?

This heading explains the working of tasks or instructions that you have just completed.

You will also find some other learning aids in the book, including:

Pop quiz – heading

These are short multiple choice questions intended to help you test your own understanding.

Have a go hero – heading

These set practical challenges and give you ideas for experimenting with what you have learned.

You will also find a number of styles of text that distinguish between different kinds of information. Here are some examples of these styles and an explanation of their meaning.

Code words in text are shown as follows: "In our game, the player will have a Score private variable to store how many enemies they stomped in that life, while a Lives global variable stores how many lives they have left before they lose."

New terms and **important words** are shown in bold. Words that you see on the screen, in menus or dialog boxes, for example, appear in the text like this: "Click on the **Application 1** node in the **Project** window."

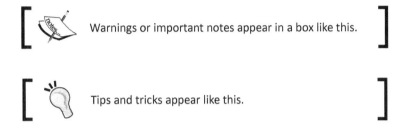

> Warnings or important notes appear in a box like this.

> Tips and tricks appear like this.

Reader feedback

Feedback from our readers is always welcome. Let us know what you think about this book—what you liked or may have disliked. Reader feedback is important for us to develop titles that you really get the most out of.

To send us general feedback, simply send an e-mail to feedback@packtpub.com, and mention the book title through the subject of your message.

If there is a topic that you have expertise in and you are interested in either writing or contributing to a book, see our author guide on www.packtpub.com/authors.

Customer support

Now that you are the proud owner of a Packt book, we have a number of things to help you to get the most from your purchase.

Downloading the example code

You can download the example code files for all Packt books you have purchased from your account at http://www.packtpub.com. If you purchased this book elsewhere, you can visit http://www.packtpub.com/support and register to have the files e-mailed directly to you.

Errata

Although we have taken every care to ensure the accuracy of our content, mistakes do happen. If you find a mistake in one of our books—maybe a mistake in the text or the code—we would be grateful if you would report this to us. By doing so, you can save other readers from frustration and help us improve subsequent versions of this book. If you find any errata, please report them by visiting `http://www.packtpub.com/support`, selecting your book, clicking on the **errata submission form** link, and entering the details of your errata. Once your errata are verified, your submission will be accepted and the errata will be uploaded to our website, or added to any list of existing errata, under the Errata section of that title.

Piracy

Piracy of copyright material on the Internet is an ongoing problem across all media. At Packt, we take the protection of our copyright and licenses very seriously. If you come across any illegal copies of our works, in any form, on the Internet, please provide us with the location address or website name immediately so that we can pursue a remedy.

Please contact us at `copyright@packtpub.com` with a link to the suspected pirated material.

We appreciate your help in protecting our authors, and our ability to bring you valuable content.

Questions

You can contact us at `questions@packtpub.com` if you are having a problem with any aspect of the book, and we will do our best to address it.

1

Our First Look at Construct

In this book, we will be learning to use Construct Classic, a free open source 2D game creator. However, before we start making games, we'll need to know how to use the tool itself.

In this chapter, we shall:

- ◆ Download and install the latest version of Construct Classic
- ◆ Create a new game project
- ◆ Learn to navigate around the interface of Construct Classic
- ◆ Learn to work with objects

So let's get on with it.

The first step: downloading and installing Construct Classic

Before we start using Construct, we need to get it running. In this part of the chapter, we'll be visiting the *Scirra* website to download a copy of Construct Classic, and then we'll go through the steps for installing it. If you already have Construct Classic installed, you can skip this step.

Time for action – getting Construct Classic up and running

Following these steps will lead to an installation of Construct Classic ready to go. To do this, you'll need access to the Internet and the Microsoft Windows operating system on the computer you're installing Construct on.

1. First, navigate your web browser to www.scirra.com. This is the home page of Construct Classic and Construct 2.

2. Click on the **Make Games** tab, and choose the subtab **Construct Classic**.

3. Next, scroll down and click on **Download Construct Classic R1.2**. This may change to newer versions of Construct Classic in future, but the link position will be the same. Click on the link to start your download.

4. After downloading the installer, double-click to start the installation process.

5. Click through the installer pages until finally presented with the option to begin installation.

6. After the installation, the Visual Studio runtime will be installed along with the latest version of DirectX (downloaded automatically).

7. The installation should now be complete, and Construct Classic is ready to load!

Step two: creating a game project

Now that Construct is installed, we will learn how to make a game (Direct-X) project after we first launch it.

Creating a project is the first step in making any game in Construct, but for now, we will create one to set us up for learning to navigate the interface.

Time for action – starting a game project

We are going to make a blank game project to allow us to navigate all areas of Construct.

1. Open up Construct and click **File** | **New** | **New Direct-X game**. This menu option is shown in the following screenshot:

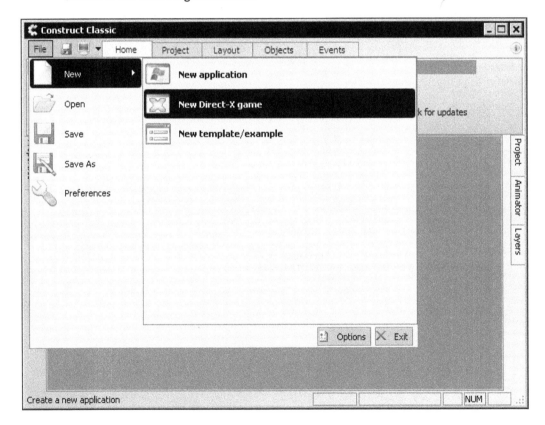

2. We now have a project. Click on the **Application 1** node in the **Project** window. The display should now look similar to the following screenshot:

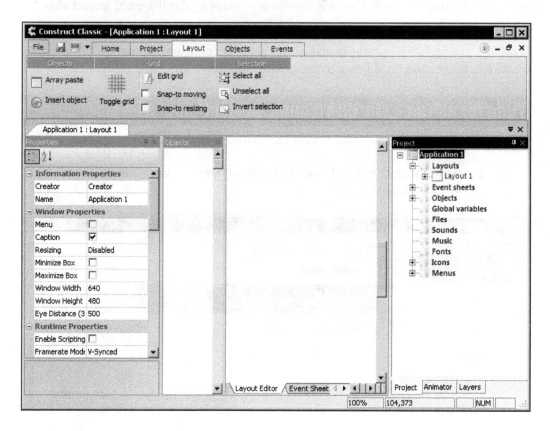

3. For this chapter, we're just going to change the **Creator** and the **Name** boxes. Go ahead and type your name into the **Creator** box and My Game into the **Name** box.

4. Now, we're going to test if the project works. Click on the **Project** ribbon button (shown in the following screenshot), and then click on the **Run All** button underneath it to start your game:

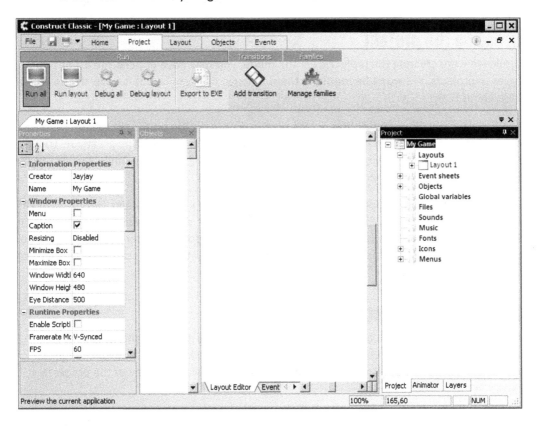

5. We now have the pop-up window, which looks similar to the following screenshot. It doesn't look like much, but this is the starting point we will use to find our way around the interface of Construct Classic. Click the **x** button to close the window.

What just happened?

We've just learned how to create a blank game project file in Construct, give it a name, and run our entire game. These steps will be used again each time we start a blank game project.

Creating the project

While we were creating the project from the menu, you may have noticed the other two types of projects. We won't be requiring them to make our games, but it is worth knowing a little about them.

The first option is **New Application**, which creates a program that does not rely on Direct-X, and rather uses the built-in rendering used by Windows. This project type greatly restricts the plugins that can be used, and is not intended for creating games. As such, we will not use this application project type in this book.

The third option, **New Template/Example**, is a collection of starter projects and tutorials that can make creating games of certain genres easier. The most playable template included is the Ghost Shooter tutorial, which includes a fully-working top-down shooter to start with. In our case, however, we will be creating all of our games from scratch, so we can make all kinds of games from the ground up.

Changing the project details

Although our interaction in this step was basic, we caught a glance of all the options available for defining the project. For now, all we needed to know was how to change the name and the creator of the game, but later on, we'll be revisiting many of the properties shown in
that list.

Running the project

In this final step, we learned how to start our game up. This step is fairly straightforward, but it is worth noting that another way to click on **Run All** is to click the small monitor icon next to the save icon.

Have a go hero – try again from memory

Now that we've learned how to create blank projects, try it again to see if you can remember how to do it.

Step three: navigating the interface of Construct Classic

Now that we have Construct Classic and a game project set up, we can explore all the areas of the Construct editor that we need to learn, to make games. For now, we are going to have a glance around the editor.

Time for action – clicking our way around Construct Classic

Using the game project from the previous exercise, we are now going to click through and look at various windows we'll be revisiting many times throughout the book.

1. Start a new blank game project as we learned earlier. We start the project in the **Layout** editor tab. By clicking the pin button on the **Properties** and **Project** boxes, they will minimize to the sides of the screen to provide more viewing area. It is also possible to resize these panels by holding the cursor over the edges of the boxes and clicking to drag their width. The following screenshot shows these buttons with arrows:

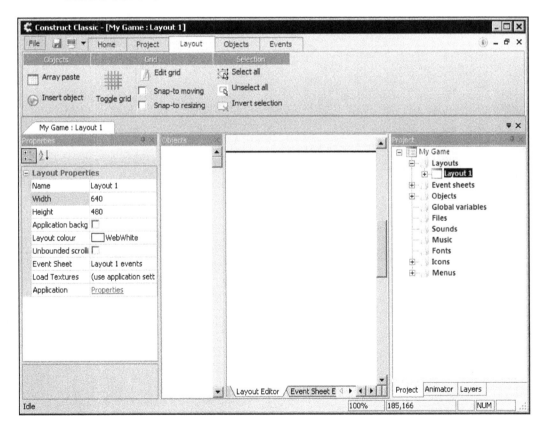

2. Now click on the **Event Sheet Editor** tab to reach the view shown in the following screenshot. Notice that the ribbon bar automatically switches to the **Events** tab to provide some quick options.

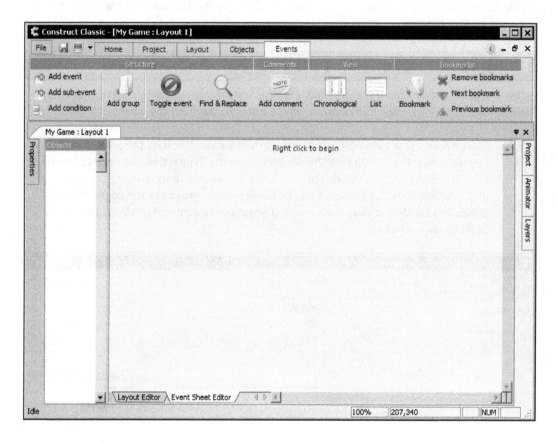

3. Now that we've visited both the event editor and layout editor, we can look at the boxes on the right side of the editor. We've already met the **Properties** box on the left-hand side, so now if the right box is minimized as shown in the previous screenshot, click on the pin button again to display it. You should see the following screenshot:

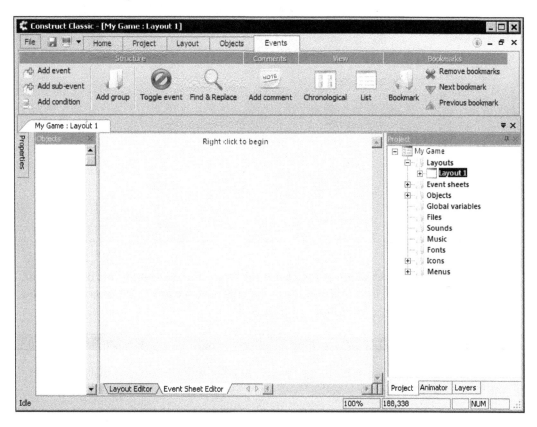

4. Clicking on the **Animator** tab will show the animation box. It will be blank, as shown in the following screenshot, as we do not have an animated object to select yet:

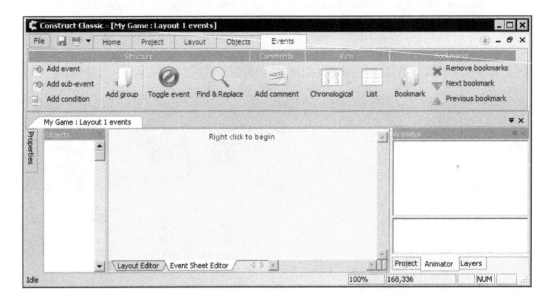

5. Finally, we can take a look at the **Layers** tab to see the different layers of our layout. Once again, there isn't much to see as we only have a blank game project right now, as in the following screenshot:

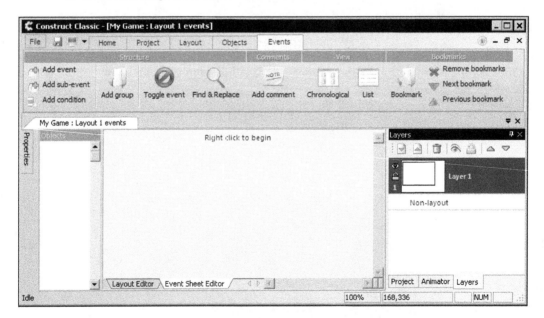

What just happened?

We've now learned to switch between the different views of the editor. Now, we can look more closely at what options are available for them.

The layout editor

This is the area that is used to create and modify the objects that make our games. Most changes made here are directly visible when the game is run.

The properties box

This box is used to modify the settings and values for most selectable items in Construct Classic. We will be using it frequently to make games throughout the book.

The event editor

In this area, we can create the rules for our games through conditions that trigger actions. An example of a condition is when a player touches a harmful substance (such as lava), we can make an event that checks for this condition and then triggers an action that removes a life from the player's lives variable.

The animator box

This box is used to create graphics and animations for our game objects the player will be interacting with.

The layers box

The layers box allows the organization of objects into different layers. This is useful for creating objects that scroll at different speeds to create a parallax effect, as well as a separate foreground and background objects. Layers can be hidden by clicking the eye icon, and locked by clicking the lock icon, as shown in the following screenshot. They can also be named in the **Properties** box.

The eye and the lock icon are found by default (visible and unlocked) on the left of each layer.

The final step: an introduction to objects

To finish the chapter, we are going to look at what objects are and what some of them do. Objects are the most important part of making a game in Construct as they usually interact directly with the player.

Time for action – creating some objects

We are now going to place some objects in the layout and modify their properties.

1. Open your blank game project from last time, or if you feel like getting some more practice, create a new one.

2. Right-click inside the layout editor, and click the **Insert an object** option shown in the following screenshot. This can also be done by double-clicking on a blank space of the layout.

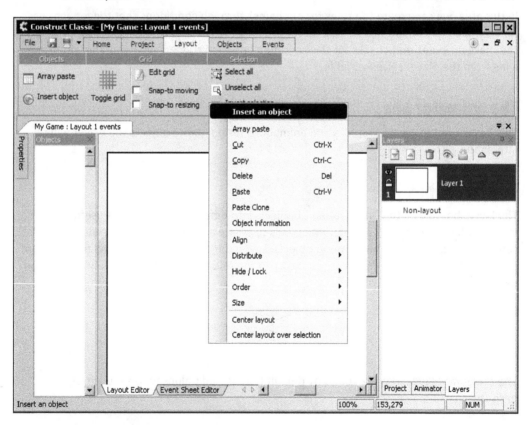

3. We now have the following object creation box where we can see all the types of objects we can insert into the layout. These are pre-programmed objects created in C++. Select the **Sprite** object and click on **Insert**. This can also be performed by double-clicking the **Sprite** object. Now, we can click inside the layout to place the sprite object.

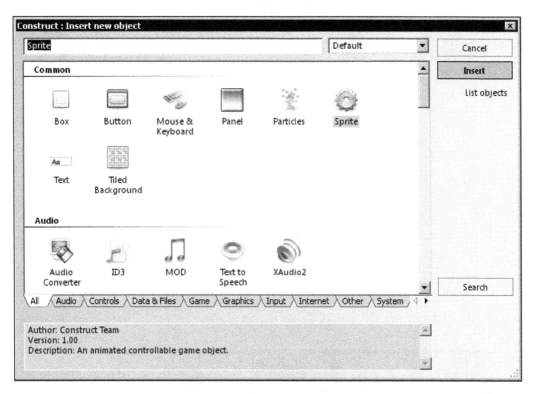

4. We are then shown an image editor for our sprite. For now, we will make a simple square graphic as shown in the following screenshot. To do this, click the paint bucket, choose a color, and then click an empty space in the graphic space.

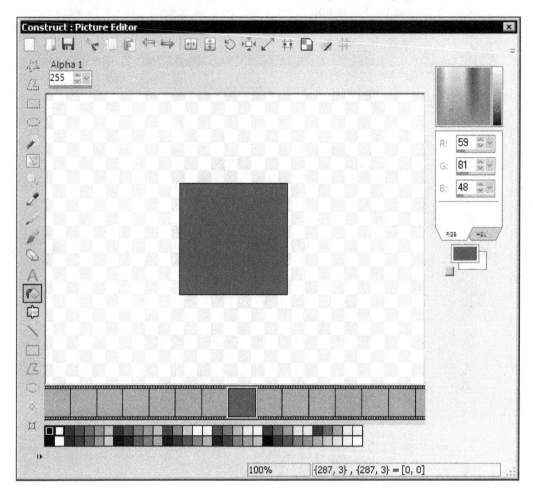

5. Now, click the **x** button to return to the layout editor. Click on **Yes** when asked to save, and we will now have a sprite in our layout as shown in the following screenshot:

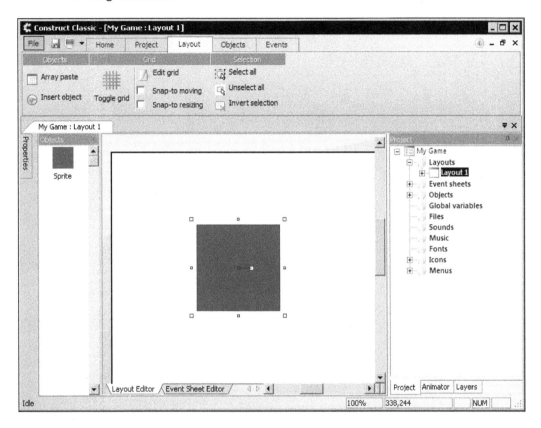

6. We can use the white box in the middle to change the angle of our sprite and the boxes on the edge of the sprite to change its size. Try matching the following shape:

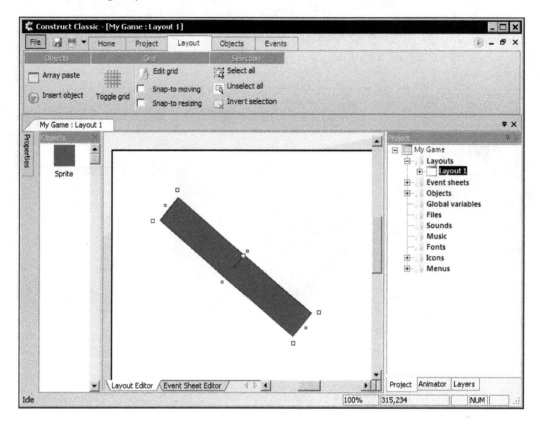

7. Now, open the **Properties** box on the left side, and scroll down to the option **Make 1:1** in the **Properties** group. Clicking on this will make our sprite return to normal size again, as in the following screenshot:

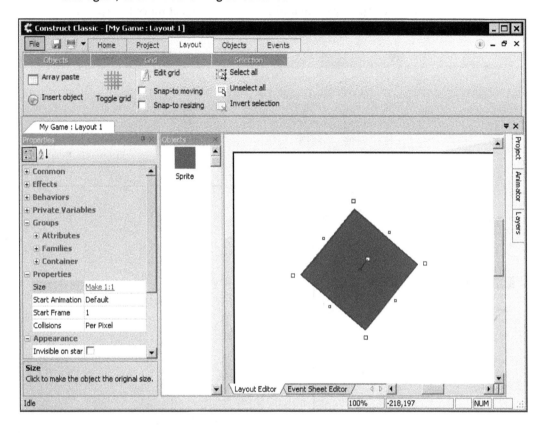

8. We now know how to resize and rotate the sprite object. We can also do this by modifying the values in the **Common** group. Open this group and try changing the **X**, **Y**, **Width**, **Height**, **Angle**, and **Opacity** fields to see what they change. It is worth noting that a lower opacity value makes the sprite object more transparent, and recently changed values will be shown in bold.

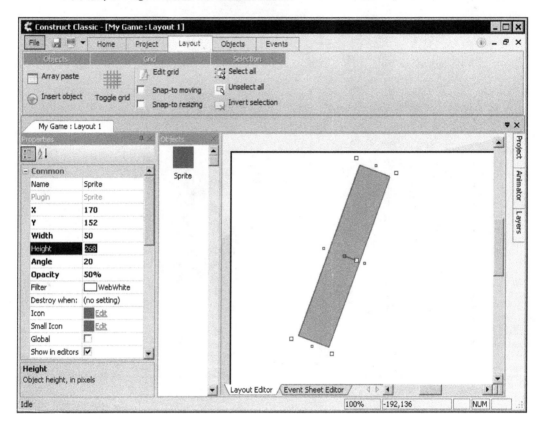

9. We can also give our sprite object a name just by changing the **Name** box. This is useful, as later we will be using many different sprite objects to create our games. For now, scroll down in the **Properties** box to view another group called **Appearance**; toying around with the values **Skew X** and **Skew Y** produces distortions, shown in the following screenshot. Notice that the selection box for the sprite does not skew with the sprite itself.

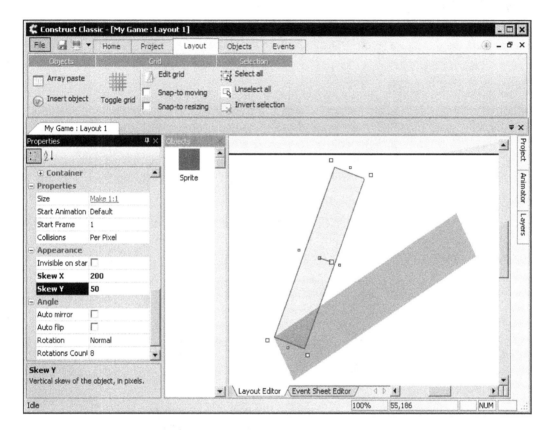

10. We can also tick the **Invisible on start** checkbox. This lets the graphic be shown in the editor, but hidden when the game is run. This is good for making invisible walls and other such objects.

What just happened?

We have now just learned to create objects such as sprites, move them around, and modify their appearance using the editor. Let's look at the different subtasks we went through to do this.

Creating an object

We learned how to bring up the object creation box and then insert a sprite into our layout. Every object we put into a layout is available in this dialog box.

Drawing the sprite

Although we only had a quick interaction with the graphic editor, we saw where our graphic files are drawn and modified. If we wanted, we could even copy-and-paste graphics from other drawing programs into the editor. It's worth noting that some painting programs may copy images differently than Construct Classic expects. Should this happen, pasting into Microsoft Paint first and then transferring that image to Construct will avoid these problems, but will not keep alpha levels.

Each drawing tool that we can use in Construct Classic has a brief informative message in the bottom-left corner of the graphic editor to explain its purpose. However, let's take a look at some of the other controls used to draw graphics in Construct:

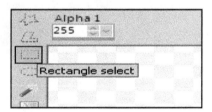

- The **Rectangle select** tool, as shown in the previous screenshot, is used to drag-and-select rectangular chunks of our graphics to move, rotate, scale, cut/delete, copy, paste, change the color of, and flip.

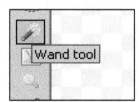

◆ The **Wand tool**, as shown in the previous screenshot, is used to automatically select parts of the graphic that touch and have similar colors. Holding *Shift* and clicking will select all parts of the graphic with similar colors regardless of whether or not they are touching.

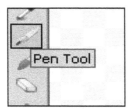

◆ The **Pen Tool**, as shown in the previous screenshot, lets us draw on our graphic as if we were using a pencil.

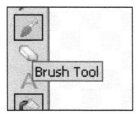

◆ The **Brush tool**, as shown in the previous screenshot, is similar to the Pen tool, except it has a much larger amount of options that can be changed using the sliders.

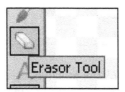

◆ The **Erasor Tool**, as shown in the previous screenshot, is used to erase and has the same options as the Brush Tool.

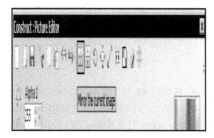

◆ The **Mirror** tool, found at the top of the window, as shown in the previous screenshot, is used to flip an image or selection horizontally.

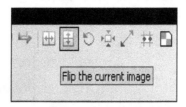

◆ The **Flip** tool is used to vertically flip the image or selection.

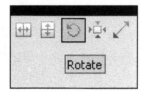

◆ The **Rotate** tool, as shown in the previous screenshot, provides a choice of angles for the image or selection to be rotated.

◆ The **Crop** tool is used to shrink the editable region of the graphic (the canvas) to fit the graphic. Use this if you draw something smaller than the boundaries.

◆ The **Resize Canvas** tool, as shown in the previous screenshot, is used to increase or decrease the size of the canvas by showing a pop-up box that lets you input a new height and width for the canvas. The drawing itself is not resized, however.

Changing the appearance of the sprite

We then learned how to modify our sprite using stretches, skews, and rotations. Changes we made here are shown when we run the game.

Have a go hero – make a picture of sprites

Now that we have gone through the process to create a sprite, try adding some more to form a picture from them. If you are stuck thinking of ideas, then try some of these:

◆ A house made up of separate sprites for the roof, base, windows, and door

◆ A magician with additional sprites for a staff and a wizard hat

◆ A car with sprites for the tires and a body sprite

 If you wish to draw the images using another paint program that does not support transparent backgrounds, use the RGB color (255,0,255) as your background color. In Microsoft Paint, this color is the brightest shade of pink in the default palette.

Summary

This chapter taught us a lot about navigating around Construct Classic as well as creating objects that we'll be using to make games.

Specifically, we went through the steps to install a fresh copy of Construct Classic on our computer that we retrieved from the Scirra website. We then went on to create a new game project and looked around the various interface views of the editor. After that, we learned how to make, position, angle, and size Sprites, a key object in any games we make. To finish the chapter, we took a quick look at some of the tools we will be coming across in making our game.

We also discussed the different tools we'll be using to create images for sprites using Construct's graphic editor.

Now that we've learned about the basics of navigating and using Construct Classic, we're ready to move on to starting our first game!

2
Hello World! Construct Style

Now that we know how to navigate around the interface, we can move on to making games. The first, we'll be making is a platformer, such as the classic Mario and Sonic, the Hedgehog games.

In this chapter, we are going to:

- ◆ Learn more about sprites, as well as how they can be animated
- ◆ Learn how to use the tiled background object to make levels and backgrounds
- ◆ Learn how to set the attributes of objects
- ◆ Learn what behaviors are and how they affect objects
- ◆ Learn what private and global variables are and how to define them
- ◆ Use textboxes to display information to the player
- ◆ Use events to control the game

So let's get started!

Sprites revisited

We've already covered the creation of a sprite object in Chapter 1, *Our First Look at Construct*. We'll now learn to create animations for them and get them ready for a real game. These skills are needed for making player and enemy sprites in nearly any game made in Construct.

Time for action – creating a player sprite

We are now going to make our player object and set the animations for it.

1. Start a blank game project (similar to the one we created in Chapter 1, *Our First Look at Construct*), and give it the name `MyPlatformer`. Then enter your author name in the **Creator** box.

Downloading the example code

You can download the example code files for all Packt books you have purchased from your account at `http://www.packtpub.com`. If you purchased this book elsewhere, you can visit `http://www.packtpub.com/support` and register to have the files e-mailed directly to you.

2. Next, add a sprite into the layout.

3. We're now going to need some player graphics. You can use Construct's Picture Editor to make these or use a painting program of your choice. For this game, the player is ball-shaped and rolls around the map. It has animation frames for falling, jumping, dying, and winning a level. See the following reference image (exact image size does not matter, as the player is resized in the layout editor):

| Normal | Rolling 1 | Upside down | Rolling 2 | Falling | Dying | Winning | Jumping |

4. Now that we have these graphics ready, put/draw the first frame *Normal* into the image, and click on the **Hotspot** button (the red target icon) to set the hotspot at the bottom-center of the image, as shown in the following image. When finished with your player graphic, close the image editor, and click on **Yes** when it prompts you to save.

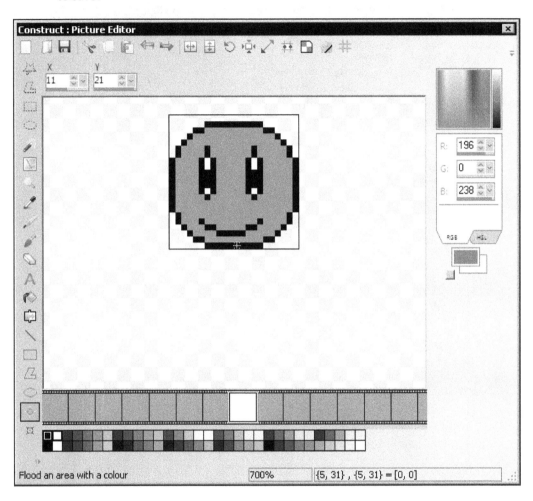

5. Now open the right-side menu to the **Animator** tab, and return to the left-side **Properties** menu. By selecting the Animation **Default** on the right menu, we can now apply a Tag to the animation using the left menu. Choose **Stopped**, as shown in the following screenshot:

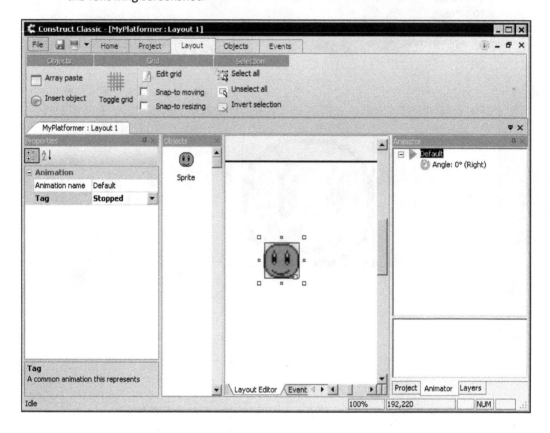

6. Now right-click on a blank area of the right menu; click and choose the option **Add new animation**. On the left side of the screen, we can now name this animation to **Rolling**. Give this animation the tag **Walking**, as shown in the following screenshot:

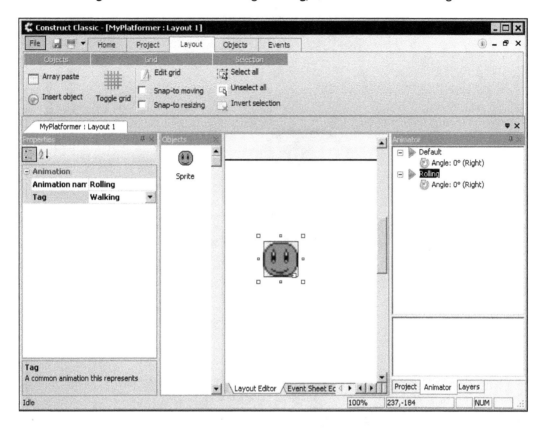

7. Now click on **Angle** underneath **Rolling**, and double-click the blank frame 1, as shown in the following screenshot, to bring up the image editor. This will be the first image in our rolling sequence.

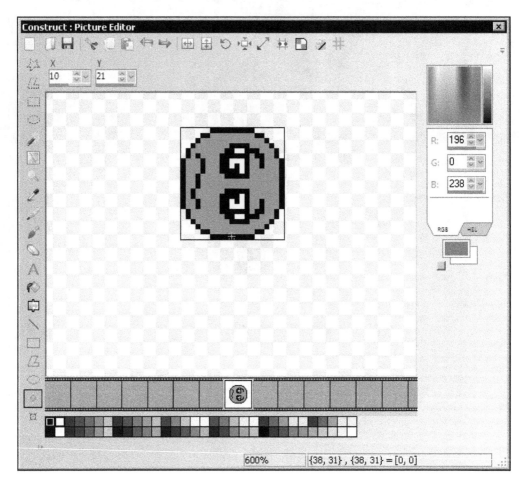

8. Now select the **Angle** again to edit the properties for that angle. We'll want the whole rolling animation to play around three times per second while the player is moving. Change the number in **Animation speed** from 50 to 3.

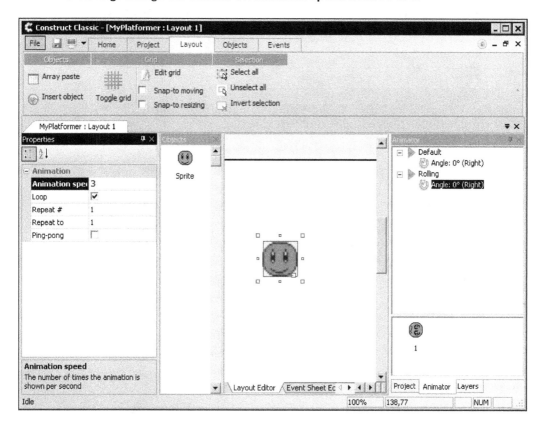

9. We can now continue adding the rest of our animation frames for **Rolling**. Right-click on the animation frames box, and click on **Add frame** from the context menu. Add the next four stages of the rolling sequence (rolling1, upside down, rolling2, and finally, normal again) into the animation so that the four animation frames are as seen in the following screenshot:

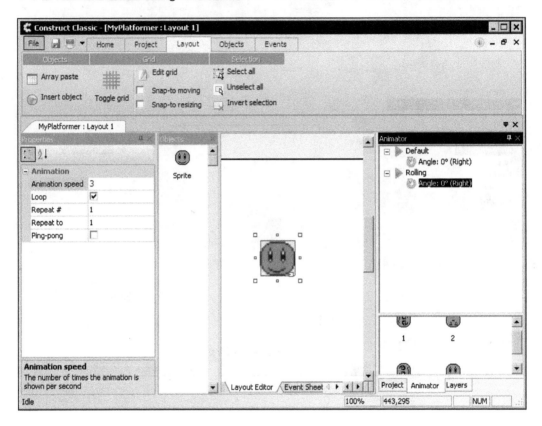

10. Now add the new animations **Jump**, **Fall**, **Die**, and **Win**, as in the following screenshot. For the **Jump** and **Fall** animations, give them the tags `Jumping` and `Falling` respectively.

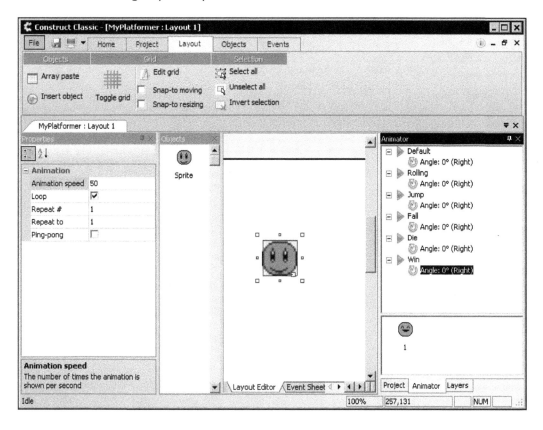

11. Next, click on your sprite, and in the top field of the **Properties** box, enter a name such as Player. Then scroll to the bottom of the **Properties** window and tick the box **Auto mirror** in the group **Angle**, as in the following screenshot:

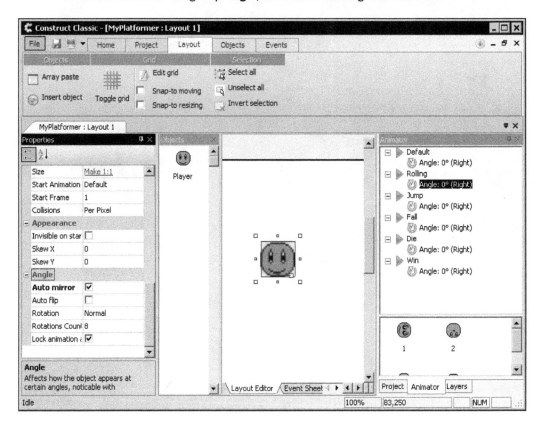

12. Finally, set the **Collisions** property of the sprite (in the **Properties** group) to **Bounding box**, as shown in the following screenshot:

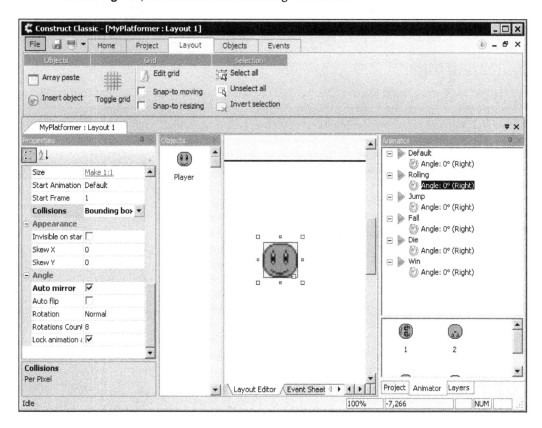

What just happened?

We now have our player sprite drawn and animated. Let's take a closer look at what we did.

Creating new animations

As seen earlier, we created a new sprite and drew a picture for it. However, this time, we went on to create multiple animations and pictures.

Each animation can have multiple angles added to it; these angles are in increments of 45 degrees and will override the default rotation method of Construct. The default angle included with every new animation is 0 degrees (the direction right).

The hotspot of an image is its centre point, where the image is rotated and positioned around. We placed it at the same point in each image to ensure that the player object doesn't *jitter* as they roll around. A quick way to put the hotspot in corners, edges, or the centre of an image is to use the number pad keys.

Animation tags

Animation tags are used in Construct's built-in movements to define which animation plays when the player is moving in a certain way. They do not affect any other animations an object has, but can override them when the player begins moving.

However, the benefit of animation tags is that they will play the correct animation when an object is moved using the pre-made movement behaviors of Construct Classic, as we will see with this first game.

Choosing the Collisions mode

The Collisions selection is used to decide when a sprite is colliding with another.

The following collision modes are available:

- **None**: In this mode, no collisions will be reported for the object
- **Point**: In this mode, there are collisions only at the hotspot point of the object
- **Bounding box**: In this mode, the object collides as if it is in a box, which stretches to its size
- **Per Pixel**: In this mode, any non-transparent pixels of the object will be checked for collisions

Although each collision mode is more complex than the previous one and will require more processing, no noticeable effect will be produced in simple games besides how the objects move around each other.

Tiled backgrounds: defining the world

If you tried making a large image out of individual tile sprites, you'd quickly tire of trying to position each one. It is equally troublesome to store a large level in a single image, as they would take up too much video memory.

This is where the tiled background comes into picture. It repeats the same graphic, for as long and wide as you stretch it. These are great for making levels and worlds!

Time for action – make some tiled backgrounds

We are now going to make two tiled backgrounds: one for the grass that our player walks along, and the other for the dirt underneath.

1. First, we'll create the grass background object. Once again, open the **Insert object** box. Instead of a sprite, insert a **Tiled Background** object from the group **Game**.

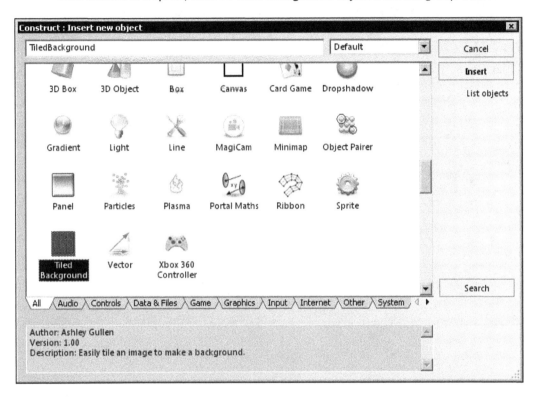

2. Now draw the image for your grass. It does not need a hotspot, as the hotspot of a tiled background is always in the top-left corner.

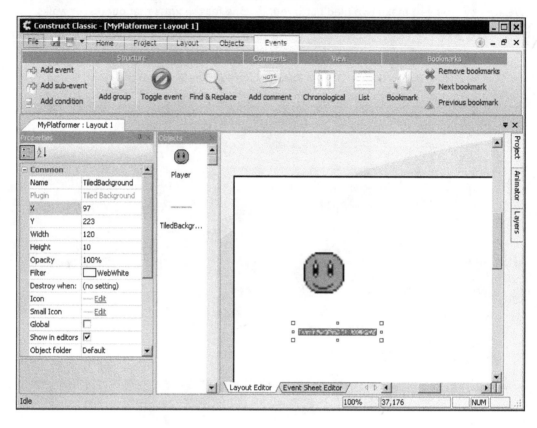

3. Now name it `Grass`, and move on to making another one called `Dirt`. Position them to form an initial platform underneath the player, as in the following screenshot:

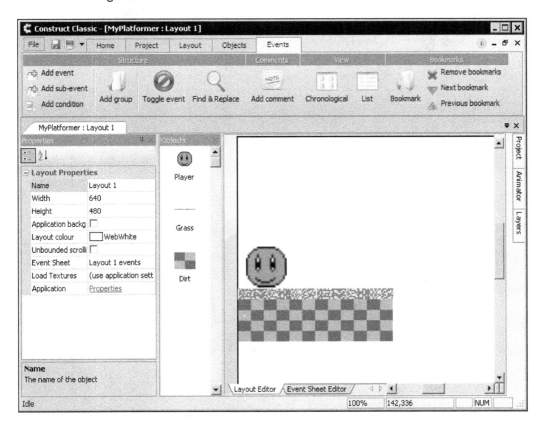

4. Change the **Width** of the layout to 1000 and the **Height** of the layout to 800. Then, make the entire level by copy-and-pasting (or dragging from the **Objects** bar) the grass and dirt objects around the layout, as shown in the following screenshot. You can use *Ctrl* and the mouse scroll wheel to zoom in and out of the layout.

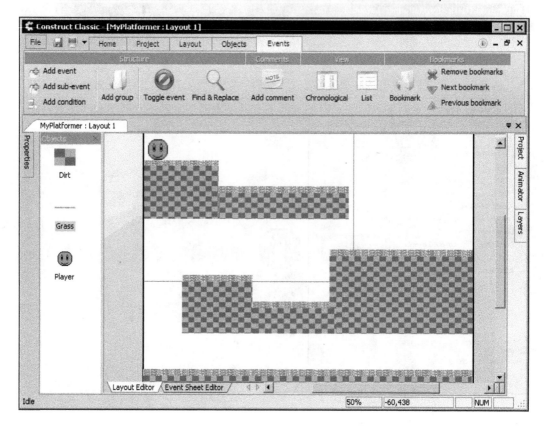

5. Finally, set the layout background color to a shade of blue for the sky. Do this by clicking on a blank space of the layout, using the **Layout colour** box in the left properties menu, as shown in the following screenshot:

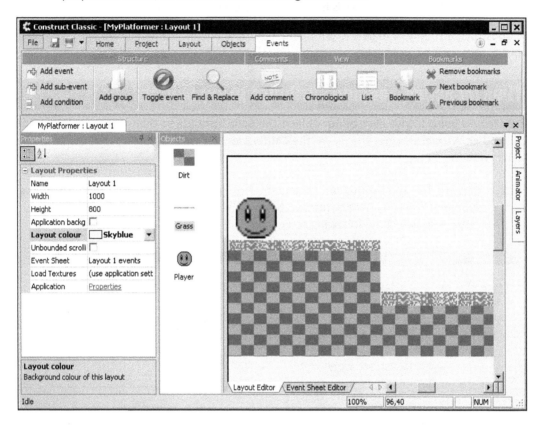

What just happened?

We have now learned how to place tiled backgrounds and make maps from them; notice how they all count as the same object. We have also learned how to change the background color of a layout.

Have a go hero – another tiled background

Using your newfound knowledge, try adding some more tiled background pieces to the map such as blades of grass or clouds in the sky. You can also go on to add background scenery. However, for non-repeating scenery such as rocks, it would be better to just make sprites.

Attributes: telling Construct more about our objects

We are now going to learn about attributes. These can be thought of as a list of features about objects. An example of this is how apples, bananas, and oranges are all fruits.

In Construct, attributes can be custom-made, but there are also some built-in ones with special uses we'll be looking at.

Time for action – adding attributes to our objects

We are now going to give each of our objects the **Solid** attribute so that they can collide with each other. We will also give the player the **Center view on me** attribute so that the screen scrolls with the player.

1. Click on the player sprite and expand the **Groups** menu. Then expand the **Attributes** submenu. We can now tick the two boxes **Solid** and **Centre view on me**. The end result is shown in the following screenshot:

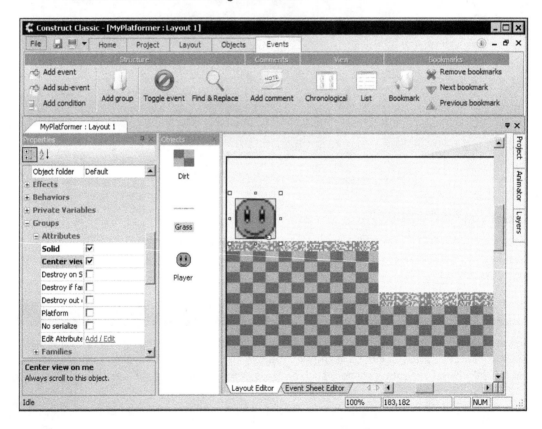

2. Now move on to give the **Solid** attribute to the grass and dirt tiled backgrounds.

3. To stop the player leaving the level, create a new tiled background called `WorldBorder` and place three of them: one for the bottom and two for the sides of the layout, as in the following screenshot. Tick **Solid** for these as well.

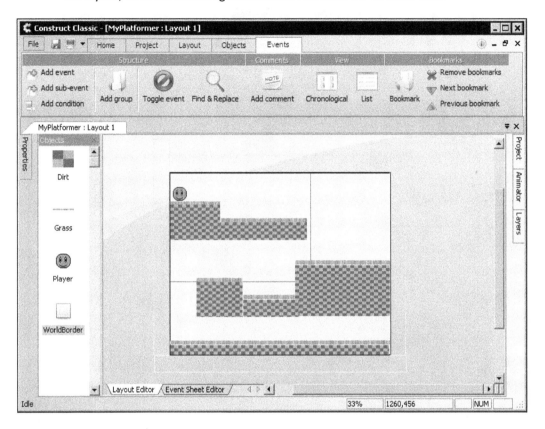

4. Finally, scroll down to the **Properties** menu (outside of **Groups**), and untick **Transparent fill** for the WorldBorder object and choose **WebGreen** as the **Fill** color. Notice in the following screenshot, the world border on the sides stretches above the level; this is to prevent the player from jumping over the wall.

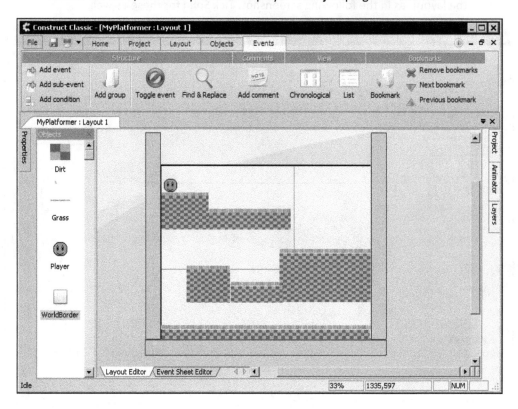

What just happened?

We've set up the attributes of our objects. Now, we can take a closer look at the other attributes in the list.

- ◆ Destroy on Startup: This attribute automatically destroys the object when the game is run. This is useful when the object is created later (for example, bullets from a gun do not *exist* until fired).

- ◆ Destroy if far: This attribute destroys the object if it is far from the layout.

- ◆ Destroy out of screen: This attribute destroys the object if it isn't in view.

- ◆ Platform: This attribute allows the object to be stood on, or jumped onto, from underneath.

- ◆ No serialize: This attribute prevents the object from being saved and loaded when using Construct's built-in *save* feature.

Behaviors: teaching objects how to act

In this segment, we'll be looking at the platform behavior and how to tweak it. Behaviors are pre-made movements and actions that an object performs in certain situations. They all have varying levels of customization, but when used correctly, can speed up game development tenfold.

Time for action – getting our player moving

Now we can give our player the platform behavior and try it out when we run the game. This is the first step in making the game interactive.

1. Select the player sprite, and scroll down the left-side menu to the **Behaviors** group. Then, click on **Add** in the **New Behavior** box. We now see the following screenshot:

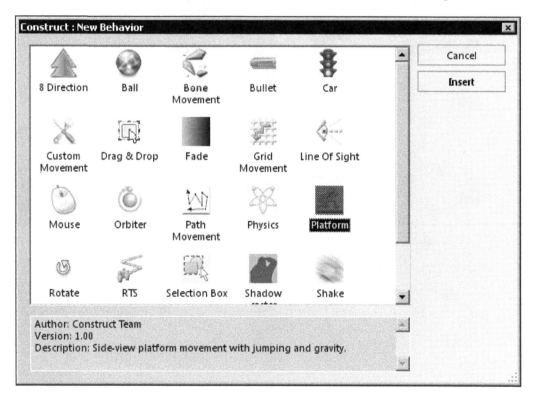

2. Our player object now has the ability to move around using the arrow keys and jump using the *Shift* key. Run the game to see this in action.

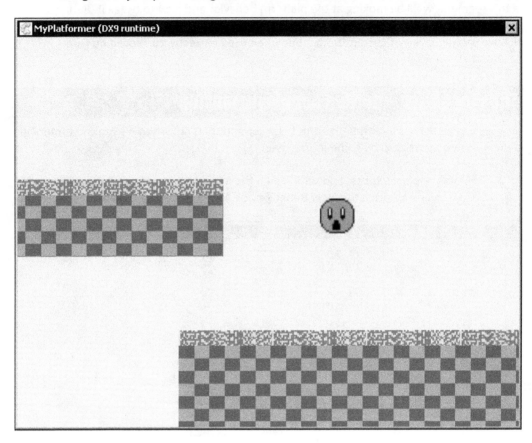

3. Now we can look at the settings for the behavior in the left screen. Change the **Jump Strength** and **Max floor speed** values, as in the following screenshot, until they control how you would want them to:

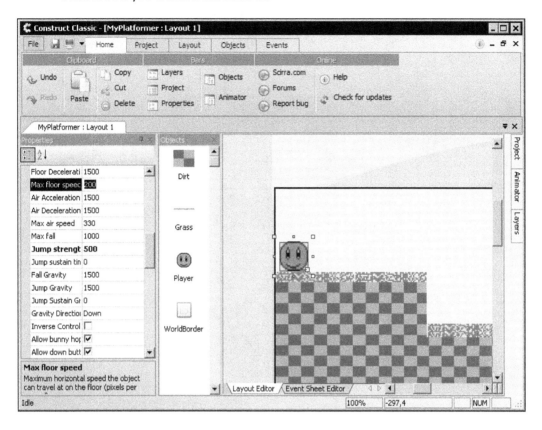

4. Finally, if you'd like to change the controls of the game, bring up the game properties menu and scroll down to the **Controls** menu. Then use the drop-down boxes to choose keys for each movement, as in the following screenshot:

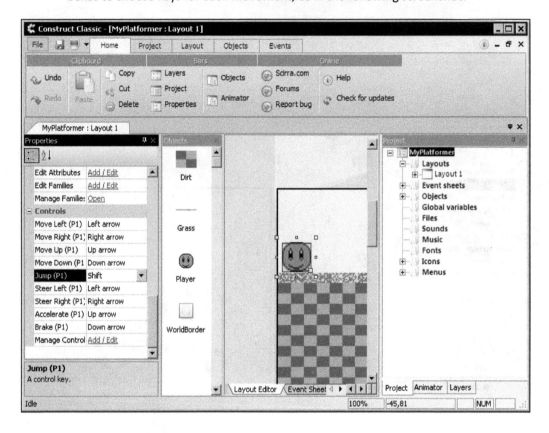

What just happened?

Our character can now move around the level at the player's wish. Let's take a look at some of the other things we caught a glimpse of.

The behaviors

We saw a large number of behaviors in the insertion box. Objects can have any number of behaviors attached to them, which in turn can be deactivated and reactivated at will. Here is a list of notable behaviors that come with Construct; more can be found on the user forums online.

- **8 Direction**: The player can travel both vertically and horizontally, usually used for top-down games.
- **Ball**: A randomly moving ball movement that can be used to produce bouncing balls, similar to the Pong game.
- **Bullet**: Gives the object (bullet) controls, such as distance and speed of fire (or instant, for realistic bullets).
- **Car**: A top-down car movement.
- **Custom Movement**: Provides the advanced settings needed to create nearly any movement type while still using Construct's built-in collision methods.
- **Grid Movement**: Forces the object to move in a grid-like fashion.
- **Physics**: Allows the object to behave with realistic motion. Objects with this behavior only collide with other objects that have it.
- **RTS**: Allows the object to be moved around obstacles using a pathfinding algorithm. As the name suggests, it is designed for **Real Time Strategy** (**RTS**) games.

Although these are only a few of them, the explanation of these and other behaviors can also be found in their descriptions.

Setting controls

It is worth noting that custom controls can be added and removed from the previous list. This is useful as controls can later be referenced by name in developing the game, but changed from a single point.

Variables: private and global

A variable is used to store a value that can change. These are useful in every game for keeping score and tracking the player's lives or health. In Construct, a private variable is stored by an object itself and can be different for each copy of that object. Meanwhile, a global variable is stored between layouts throughout the program.

Time for action – giving our player a life

In video games, a player gets a *Game Over* when the character they control runs out of lives. Right now, our player doesn't have that luxury, so let's change that. In our game, the player will have a `Score` private variable to store how many enemies they stomped in that life, while a `Lives` global variable stores how many lives they have left before they lose.

1. Open the left menu for our player again. Scroll down to the **Private Variables** group, and click on **Add/Edit** to get a window similar to the following screenshot:

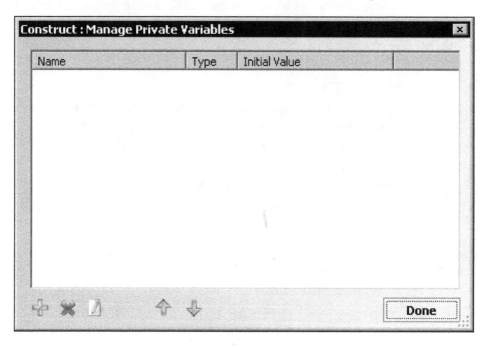

2. Now click on the plus button and create a number named `Score`. Leave the value of it at 0 and click on **OK**. Then click on **Done** in the private variable manager screen.

3. To finish, make a global variable `Lives`. To do so, open the right menu, and in the project tab, right-click on the item **Global variables** and click on the context item **Add global variable**, as in the following screenshot, when it appears:

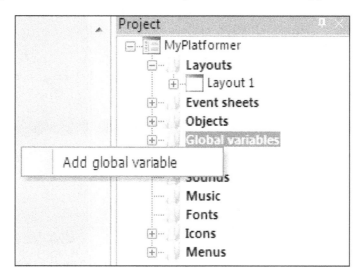

Set the value to **3** and click on **OK**, as shown in the following screenshot:

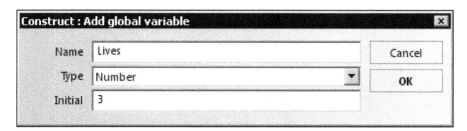

What just happened?

We have now created a private variable to store the score of the player's character for its current life and a global variable to store the number of lives they have left. Private variables are usually used to store values such as health and ammo, but can be used in situations like this where the *combo* score is more important than the total score.

Textboxes: giving the player a heads-up

Textboxes are used to write information to the player. They can tell the game story, or tell the player how they are doing. They are important in most games as they can be used to teach the player how to play, as well as guide them through the levels.

Time for action – showing our player their health and score

We are now going to make two textboxes: one is to tell the player the score, and the other is to tell the player how many lives the character they are controlling has left. We'll also learn how to keep these textboxes on the screen with the player.

1. First, we will need to add a new layer to the layout. To do this, open the **Layers** tab on the right-hand menu, and click on the upward pointing paper button to make a new top layer.

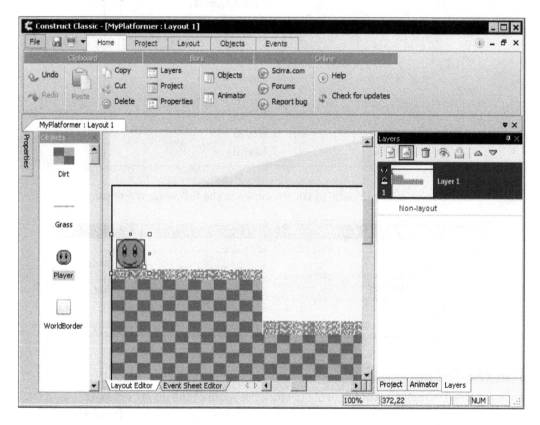

2. Layers can be modified similar to objects. Open the left menu and rename the text layer to HUD (Heads Up Display), and the other layer to Game.

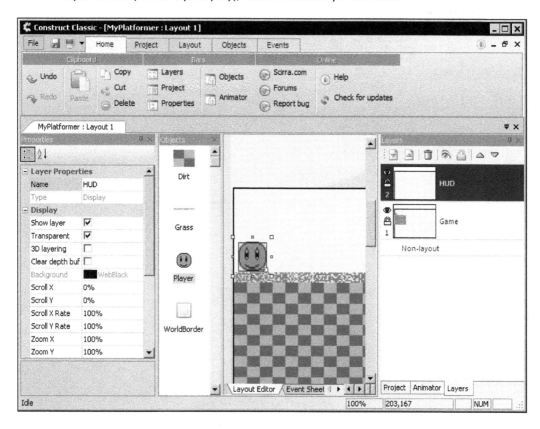

3. In the layer properties for HUD, change the `Scroll X Rate` and `Scroll Y Rate` percentages to `0`. This keeps all objects on the HUD layer in the same position on the screen while the game is running.

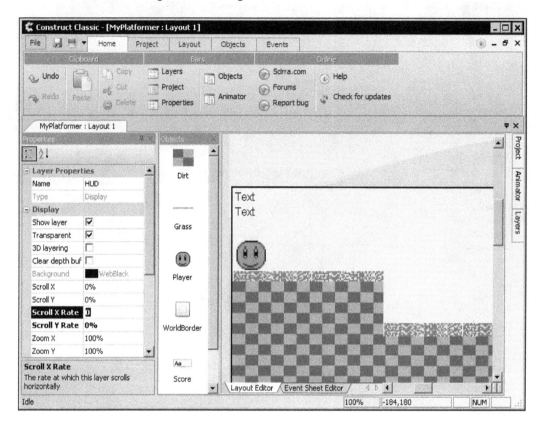

4. Now, make sure the HUD layer is highlighted, as shown in step 2. This means each object we make is created on that layer. Insert two new `Text` objects to the layout (found under the `Graphics` group).

5. We can now change the name of the first text object to `"Score"` and the second to `"Lives"`.

6. Finally, scroll down in the properties window for each textbox. Change the text of Score to "Score: 0" and the text of Lives to "Lives: 3".

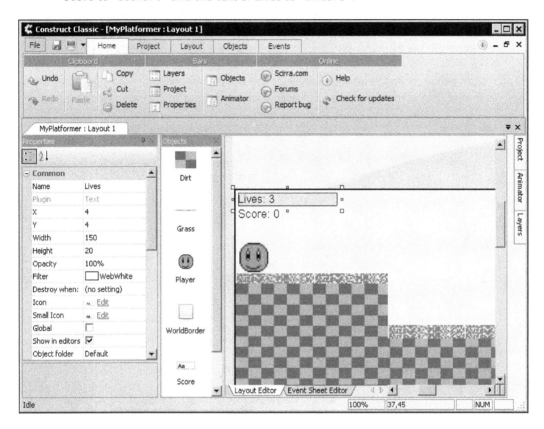

What just happened?

We now have some textboxes in our game to show the lives and score count for the player's character. We'll be linking them to the variables next through Events.

Events: setting the rules and goals of a game

We are now going to learn a little of the biggest part of game-making in Construct. Events are used to define the very logic of a game and play an integral role in complex games.

For now, we'll be learning how to use them in this game to keep their lives and score updated.

Time for action – very eventful games

When the player's character touches deadly spikes, we know they should lose health or die, but how does the game know this? That's where we are heading. First, we need to learn how to create events in the Event Sheet Editor.

1. Add a new sprite to the Game layer, which will be the end goal, and place it at the end of your level. Name it `Goal`, and give it the `Bounding box` collisions mode.

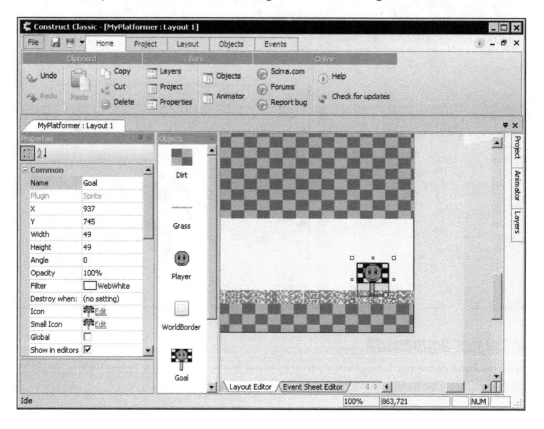

2. Now put some sprites around your level named `Hazard`. They can be lava, saw blades, spikes, or any other contraption you can think of. However, this time they will keep `Per Pixel` collisions mode.

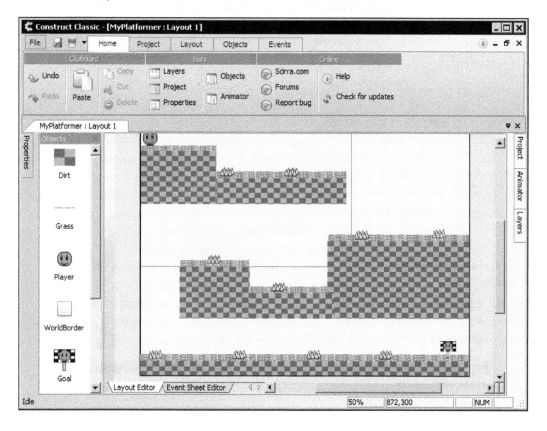

3. Now we are ready to switch to the **Event Sheet Editor** tab. Right-click while in the **Event Sheet Editor**, and click on **Insert event** in the context menu that appears.

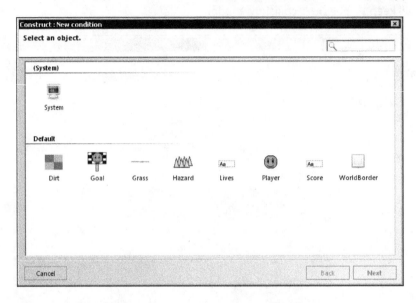

4. Each object can have its own conditions, but for now we are going to create an Always condition from the menu opened by double-clicking on the System object. The System object is included in every game.

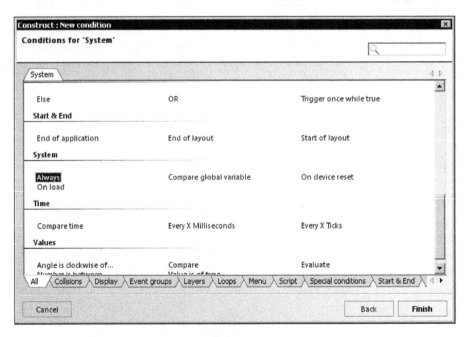

5. We now have an `Always` condition. Conditions affect when events trigger and start the actions on the right. Currently, there are no actions triggered by the `Always` condition.

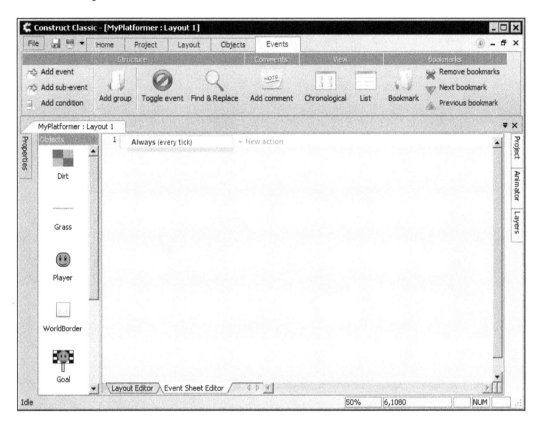

6. Click on `New action` text to bring up a menu very similar to the condition choice screen. However, this menu is used to choose what happens when the conditions of the event are all true (as an event can have more than one condition).

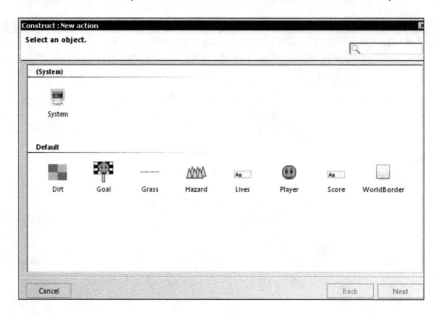

7. Now double-click on the **Lives** textbox to get to its actions list. Choose the action **Set Text**.

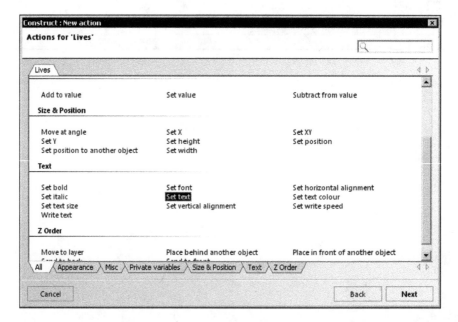

8. We are now shown an entry screen, which is expecting us to enter the text we want to display. For displaying our text, we will start with `"Lives: "`, and then display the global variable, which is accessed by typing `global('Lives')`. This makes the final string `"Lives: " & global('Lives')` (as the & symbol joins the two together).

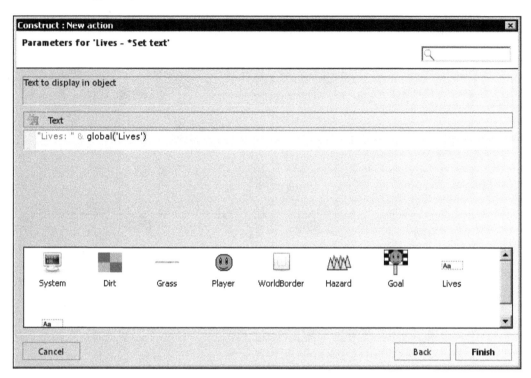

9. We now have the Lives textbox updated. Repeat the steps previous, but enter
`"Score: " & Player.Value('Score')` in the textbox. This is how private
variables are addressed.

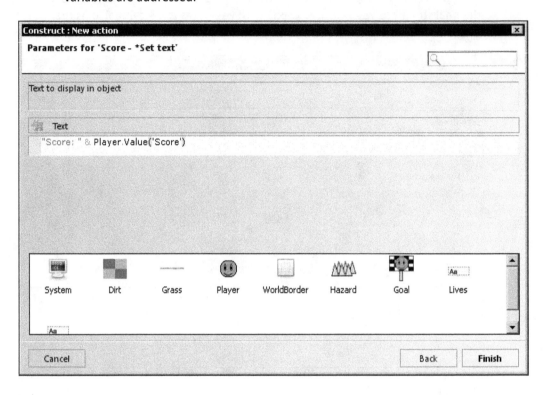

10. We now have our event to update both textboxes. Try changing the values in the editor to show they work.

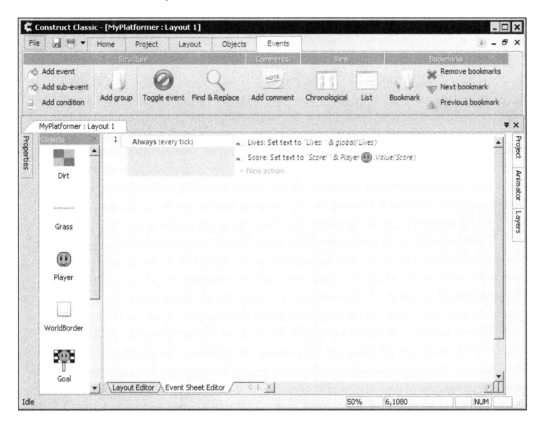

What just happened?

Events are the backbone of games made in Construct and as such will take a bit longer than one chapter to learn. Luckily, we'll be learning them all throughout the book as we can't make a full game without them. Let's see what we've learned so far.

The sprites

We made the goal and hazard sprites so that we have them ready for when we make our events to control what happens when the player touches them. The goal would make the player win the level, while the hazard would kill them and take away a precious life. For now, however, they are merely graphical objects.

Events

Events are a container of conditions and actions. When the conditions are true, the actions are triggered. Any number of conditions and actions can be contained in them.

Conditions

As mentioned before, conditions are what cause the event actions to be performed. When all conditions in an event are true, the event will trigger. We have now met the `Always` condition, which will trigger always (or every tick, which is the smallest amount of time between cycles of events). Many conditions and actions will be named, or have descriptions, to help understand of their purpose. It is worth noting that an event with no conditions is treated as having an `Always` condition.

Actions

Actions are used to cause changes, whether value, graphical, or both. They can only be performed when the event is triggered.

Summary

Now that we have started learning how to make platform games, we've covered a lot of the basics needed to make one with Construct.

We started this chapter with animated sprites, which are the most important object in any graphical games made with Construct Classic. Then we learned about tiled backgrounds, which decrease the difficulty in making large maps. We then used some attributes to define which objects are solid and learned that the Player object must have the camera centered on it at all times.

After that, we gave the Player object movement with the Platform behavior, a pre-made movement designed for 2D platformer games. Our Player object then gained a personal score counter and some lives to add some challenge to the game. We then went on to add some textboxes that show the current score and lives, and then finished off the chapter with learning how to create events, the building blocks of any new gameplay elements we want to make.

Now that we've learned to do all this, we're ready to add some bad guys and make the hazards hazardous, which is the topic of the next chapter.

3
Adding the Challenge

We know that video games would not be fun if everything was easy and pointless, and so far, our platformer game has no real difficulty. Let's change that.

In this chapter, we will:

◆ Learn how to add events to win the game when touching the goal post

◆ Add events to handle player death and a *game over* when all lives are lost

◆ Add an enemy object, and learn how to give it a mind of its own

◆ Learn how to improve the user interface

So let's get on with it.

Before we start

In this chapter, we will be moving at a faster pace than previous chapters. It may help if you look back at *Chapter 2, Hello World! Construct Style* again before continuing.

Reaching the goal

We have our goal object in place, but the events are missing to end the level in victory for the player. Let's put them in.

Time for action – making the game winnable

Right now, the player can go past the goal post without winning the level. We are now going to put in some events to let the player win when they touch the post.

1. Open our platformer game and switch to the **Event Sheet Editor**. We are now going to add a new event. Select the **Player** object and click on **Next**. Double-clicking on the **Player** object will also give the same result.

2. We now have a series of conditions related to the player object. Choose the condition **Is overlapping another object** and click on **Next** again.

3. We are now presented with a button that says **Pick an object**. Click on the button to find the **Goal** object and then click on **OK**. End creating the condition by clicking on **Finish**.

4. Right-click on the event and click on **Insert new condition** from the context menu that appears. Select the **Player** object and choose the condition **An animation is playing**. Enter `Die` in the box and click on **Finish**. Right-click on this condition in the event, and then click on **Invert condition** from the context menu.

5. Now we need to put the actions in for the event. For the first action, choose the **Player** object and, in the following screen, click on the **Platform** tab. Then select the **Set Activated** text, as in the following screenshot:

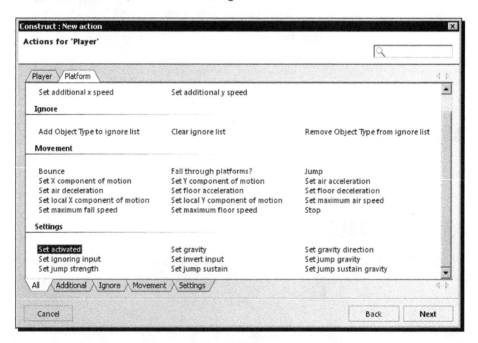

6. Clicking on **Next**, we now have an option to enable or disable the platform movement. Choose **Deactivate** and then click on **Finish**.

7. Now proceed to add yet another action to the event. Choose the **Player** object again and select **Set Animation**. In the provided textbox, enter Win as the animation name to play. Click on **Finish**.

8. Now try running the game and getting to your goal post. See if the player wins when touching the post, and then click on **X** to close the game.

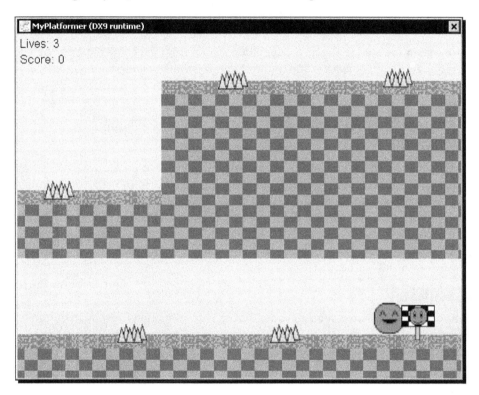

What just happened?

We now have a goal post that ends the level in victory for the player. We also created an event to handle winning the game in the future by triggering only when the player is not playing the animation Die.

We'll now take a closer look at what happened.

Overlapping versus collision

You may have noticed that there were two more collision-checking conditions available, most notably the highlighted **On collision with another object**. Overlapping will occur as long as the objects are touching, while a collision condition only triggers once when the two objects first touch. Meanwhile, the middle option **Is overlapping at offset** checks if the main object would be overlapping at a given X and Y offset.

We used overlapping instead of collision here because the player would return to their normal animations after the event triggers once. This is due to the platform movement behavior changing animations to those tagged automatically, and our event overrides this.

We were also introduced to the invert condition option from the context menu. We'll look at it in more detail in the next section, but for now, it is worth understanding that it does the opposite of what the condition normally checks for. This event is created so that in the future, when the player dies, they do not win the game while falling off the screen.

Set activated

We used the condition **Set activated** of the platform behavior to decide whether it was active or not. When disabled, no actions performed by the platform behavior are triggered, and hence the player freezes with no way to move. A condition to Activate the behavior would then return the game to normal. Note that using events to control the platform movement would bypass this and would require a check against a global variable to determine if the controls should work or not.

Set animation

Animation names are important for events that change animations. Although numbers work for referencing the animation in the list, names allow the game events to be easier to read and prevent bugs due to human error.

Avoid the hazards

Right now, we have hazards in our level that the player can just move over without any worries. We're going to change that and add some events for our lives system. This is important to make the player more cautious of moving through the level and provide an extra challenge.

Time for action – bestowing more challenges on a player

Our player is currently having no problem beating the level. Without obstacles and dangers, the game might as well just be a straight line for the player to walk down. Let's give this game some challenge.

1. Create an event that triggers when the player overlaps the Hazard object. As with touching the goal, change the player animation and deactivate the platform movement. Choose the animation Die instead this time, as in the following screenshot:

2. Now add a new event to the event sheet. Choose the Player object and select **An animation is playing** as the condition. Enter Die in the box and click on **Finish**.

3. For this event, add the action **Move at angle** for the Player object. Enter 2 as the **Pixel Distance** and **90** Degrees (downward) for the **Angle to move at**. Click on **Finish**.

4. Add one more action to the event for the `Player` object: choose **Send to front** and click on **Finish**.

5. Now insert another event for the `Player` object. Choose the condition **Object is on-screen?** and click on **Finish**. Right-click on this newly-made condition and select **Invert condition** from the context menu to negate the condition (the event now triggers when the condition is false). Notice that a not-equal sign appears before the condition.

6. Copy and paste the condition **Animation "die" is playing** from the previous event into this one. Do not negate this condition.

7. Add an action to this event for the `Player` object again. Choose the action **Destroy** and click on **Finish**.

8. Now we insert the next event by choosing the `System` object and the highlighted condition **Compare**. For the first textbox, double-click on the `Player` object and select the expression **Get number of objects**, as in the following screenshot. Click on **Finish** to end the expression.

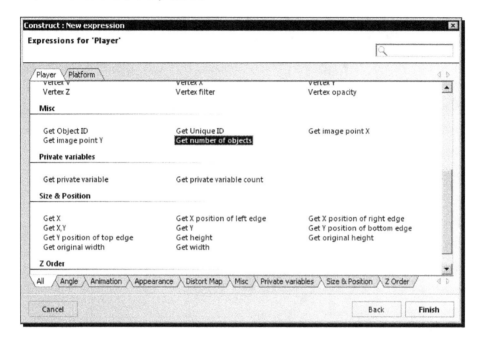

9. Leave the other textbox as **0** and click on **Finish**.

10. Now add an action for our event for the **System** object. Use the action **Subtract from value** and select the `Lives` global variable, followed by entering `1` in the box **Value**, and click on **Finish**.

11. Add another action to the event, again selecting the **System** object, and choose the action **Go to layout**. In the first box, enter the number `1`, and then in the **Duration of transition if picked, in milliseconds** box, enter `500`. Click on **Finish** to end the action.

12. Next, add another event to the event sheet. Choose the highlighted condition **Compare** from the **System** object as we did previously. Unlike last time, for the first textbox, we now double-click on the **System** object in the following box and choose the expression **Get global variable**. In the space where it says `Variable name`, enter `Lives` instead.

13. Now, in the second box, open the drop-down menu and select **Lower than**. Click on **Finish** to end the event condition.

14. Finally, give the event **System** the action `Close`, as shown in the following screenshot, and click on **Finish**:

What just happened?

We now have our lives and hazards fully working. This gives our player a chance to test their skill and makes the game playable and fun.

We'll now take a closer look at what we did.

The death of a player

We created an event that triggers when the player touches the hazards. This event caused the player to change the animation and stop moving as earlier when touching the goal post. However, we also added another event that checks what animation is currently playing for the player.

In this event, the player is moved downwards with a speed of 2 and is put in front of all other objects in the layout via the `Send to front` action. This stops the player from appearing behind the level.

We then do a final check to see if the player is no longer visible on the screen while the player is dying. If not, then the player has fallen below the level, and we can then use the `Destroy` action to remove the sprite from the layout.

Resurrecting our player

We do a check to see if the player sprite has been destroyed. If it has, we remove one life from the global variable `Lives` and restart the level again by calling layout 1. Layouts can be called by name or number, but in this instance, we only have one.

We entered a transition duration to pause the game, for half a second (500 milliseconds), before restarting the level to allow some time for the player to see what happened if they were near the bottom of the level.

Giving the player a game over

When the number of extra lives was finally lower than zero, death resulted in the game over for our player. For now, we just end the game rather than show another screen saying the game has ended. A method of displaying the game has ended would be to create a `Text` object on the HUD layer and set its text to `Game Over` instead of closing the game. You can then have a further event that will restart the layout if any key is pressed while the player lives are lower than `0`.

Putting some bad guys in

Enemies play a major role in many games and provide a feeling of joy to the player who defeats them. Right now, our player can memorize the path to take through the map and still get to the goal without much difficulty. Let's bring the challenge level up by adding in some enemies of our own.

Time for action – adding an enemy and making him move

For the player to have some challenge, we are going to add a new enemy sprite into the game and give it some intelligence to move around the level. We'll also be giving the player some score points for jumping on the heads of the enemies.

1. In the **Layout Editor**, make a new sprite for your enemy object and draw some graphics for it. Use the following graphics as reference:

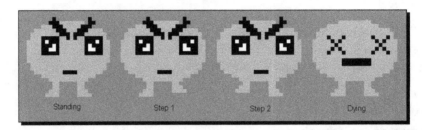

2. Add two more animations for this sprite, as we learned in the previous chapter. The first additional animation is the `Walking` animation, which has frames `Step 1`, `Standing`, `Step 2`, `Standing`, and has no tag (as it will not use any behaviors). The second animation is the `Die` animation and requires no extra frames or settings. Remember to set the animation speed of the `Walking` animation.

3. Now that our enemy sprite is animated, open its left-side Properties menu and change its name to `BadGuy`, then add the private variables **Speed** and **Direction**. Set the default value of **Speed** to 2 and the default value of **Direction** to 1.

4. Place some of the enemies around your level, as shown in the following screenshot, and return to the **Event Sheet Editor** view:

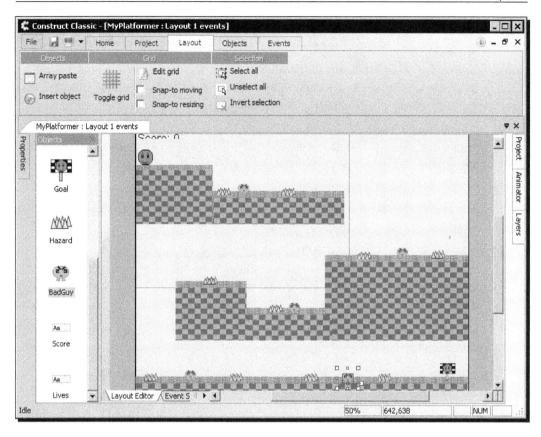

5. Now right-click on the **Always** event and choose **Insert sub-event** from the context menu. Select the **BadGuy** object and insert the condition **An animation is playing** and the animation Die. Click on **Finish** and then invert the condition.

6. We will now create some basic Enemy AI for our game. To start, add an action to the sub-event for the **BadGuy** object. Choose **Move at angle**, and in the first box, enter the private variable Speed of the Badguy (using the expression editor, or by typing BadGuy.Value('Speed') manually).

7. For the second box, enter the direction variable of the BadGuy and multiply it by 180 (`BadGuy.Value('Direction') * 180`), then click on **Finish**.

8. Now add another sub-event to the **Always** event. Select the **BadGuy** object and its condition **Is overlapping another object**. Click on **Next** and choose the object **Grass** before clicking on **Finish**. Invert this condition.

9. Add the action **Move at angle** for the **BadGuy** object to this sub-event, and set the distance to `BadGuy.Value('Speed') + 1` and angle to 90. Click on **Finish** to end the action.

10. Create another sub-event for when the BadGuy object overlaps a Grass object; do not invert it. Add the action **Set Y** for the BadGuy object and enter the value `Grass.Y`.

11. Now add another sub-event for the BadGuy object. Choose the highlighted condition **Compare a private variable** to check if the **Speed** variable is **Not equal to** the value **0**. Then add another condition to check if the BadGuy animation `Walking` is playing. Invert this condition.

12. For this sub-event, add the action `Set animation for BadGuy`, and set the animation to `"Walking"`.

13. Add a new event to the event sheet and select the **BadGuy** object. This time, choose the highlighted condition **On collision with another object**. Select the object **Dirt** and click on **Finish**.

14. Now insert the condition **OR** from the **System** object to the event. Underneath this condition, add a final collision condition and choose the object **WorldBorder**.

15. Add a sub-event for the **BadGuy** object and choose the highlighted condition **Compare a private variable**. Choose **Direction** from the drop-down list and click on **Finish**.

16. Add the highlighted action **Set value** for the **BadGuy** object and set the variable **Direction** to 1. Click on **Finish** to end the action.

17. Now right-click on the collision event and add another sub-event. Choose the **System** object and the condition **Else**.

18. In this sub-event, add the highlighted action **Set value** for **BadGuy** again, but this time, set the value of **Direction** to 0.

19. Now, add a new event for the `BadGuy` object with the condition **Is overlapping another object**, and choose the `Player` object.

20. Add a condition to this with the highlighted **Compare** condition of the `System` object. In the first box, enter `BadGuy.Y - (BadGuy.Height / 1.5)`, and use the **Comparison** mode **Greater or equal** to compare against the second value **Player.Y**, then click on **Finish**.

21. Insert another condition, this time to check if the `BadGuy` is playing the animation `Die`. Invert the condition.

22. Add a final condition to this event named **Trigger once while true** from the `System` object conditions list.

23. Create actions for this event to set the animation of the **BadGuy** to `"Die"` and the **Speed** private variable of the **BadGuy** to `0`.

24. Next, add the action **Add to value** for the `Player` object and enter the value `1` for the variable **Score**.

25. To end the event, add the action **Bounce** from the **Platform** tab of the `Player` object.

26. Add another event with the first three conditions of the last. However, change the **Compare** condition from **Greater or equal** to **Lower than**.

27. For this event, add the same actions that occur when the player touches a hazard. **Deactivate** the platform movement and change the player animation to `"Die"`.

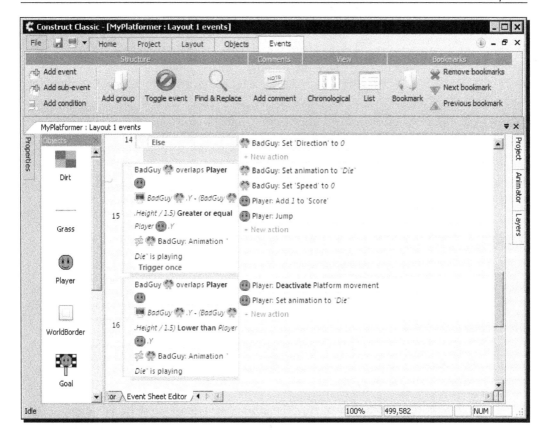

What just happened?

We've just learned how to add a basic enemy into our game. The enemy moves in a single direction until it hits a wall and then starts walking the other way. It also falls between platforms when there are no edges to bounce off.

We then added some events to allow the player to jump on their heads to attack them, or die when touched by one.

Now let's take a closer look at what happened.

Direction of motion

We used the action `Move at angle` in order to move the enemy objects without a behavior attached to them. As we saw, the action can be used multiple times in the same cycle (tick) without overriding the last call (as the enemy moved diagonally while falling, rather than straight horizontal or vertical).

Falling down

When the `BadGuy` object steps off an edge, he falls at a speed that is 1 greater than his horizontal speed. This makes for a slightly more realistic fall than if he fell at movement speed.

Turning around

When the enemy touches a wall or border, it changes `Direction` value between 1 (180 degrees, or left) and 0 (0 degrees, or right).

Looking for a hit

When the enemy touches the player, we check if the player is higher than just below the top of the enemy (through finding the lowest point `BadGuy.Y` and rising up by `BadGuy.Height` divided by `1.5`).

When the player is higher than the enemy, the player gets a score point for defeating the bad guy, who is left stunned as to how they died. However, in the opposite situation, the enemy wins and takes one of the player's precious lives.

Have a go hero – gaining lives

Using a `Compare` event, check when the player has a score greater (or equal) to `10`. If so, then add `1` to the global variable `Lives` and remove `10` from the player's score. This rewards the player for their high score by giving them an extra life. In classic platform games, a game over meant starting from the beginning of the whole game, so extra lives were invaluable for completing the game.

Improving our interface

The **Graphical User Interface** (**GUI**) is all that a player has to see their stats and is one of the most important designs to make in a game. It needs to be clear, unobtrusive, and easy to understand. Right now, our GUI is just text over whatever the screen shows, but this can be troublesome if the text is over a black area. Let's fix that.

Time for action – creating a background for the GUI

We want the text displayed to the player to have a consistent background to reduce strain on the eyes of our player. We'll do this using a Panel, an object which can be used for more complex boxes.

1. In the **Layout Editor**, select the HUD layer and insert a `Panel` object from the object group `Game`.

2. Right-click on the **Panel** and choose **Order | To Back** from the context menu. Then drag the panel behind the existing text on the HUD and stretch it to cover the text in front of it. Name the object `TextBack`, and then switch back to the **Event Sheet Editor**.

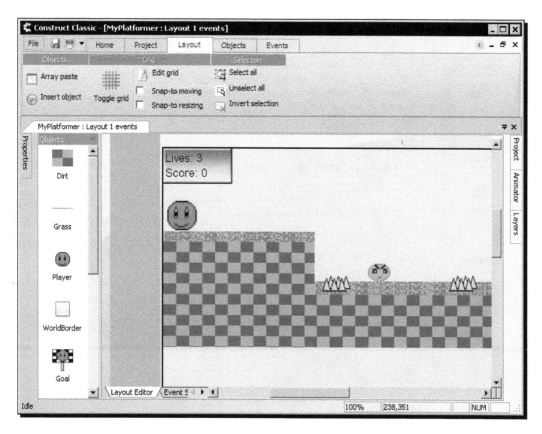

3. Now add an event to the event sheet and select the object `Player`. Use the condition **Is overlapping another object** to check if it is behind the `Panel` object.

4. Create the action `Set opacity` from the `System` object. Enter `HUD` in the first box, followed by `70` in the second.

5. Now add another event underneath and give it the `System` condition `Else`. For this event, add the same action as the previous one, but with the opacity value of `100` instead.

6. Now run the game to test if everything works as expected. Here are two images to show both how the HUD should look and how the game should look while playing. The following screenshot shows the HUD becoming transparent, as it should:

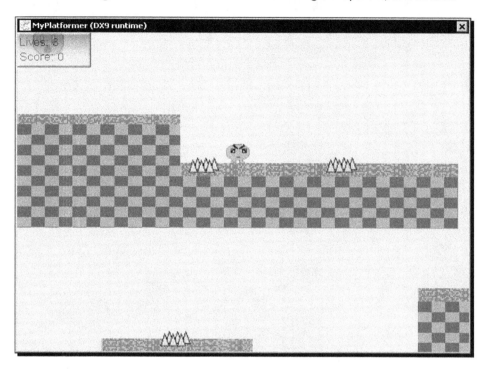

Meanwhile, the HUD will return to normal when the player is not overlapping it, as in the following screenshot:

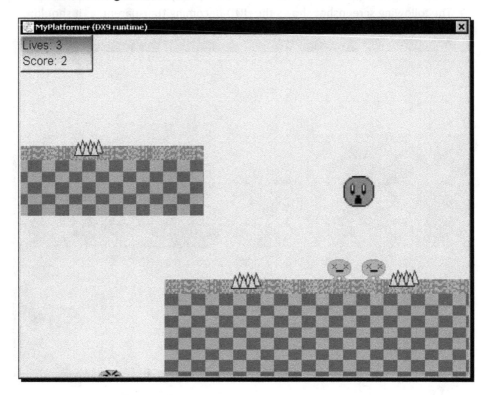

What just happened?

We've now finished the chapter by adding a panel to our textboxes. This keeps them visible and easy to see for the player. Panels can be stretched without causing the borders of the image to stretch and fray. This makes them great for games where a HUD has a plain image stretched across the middle, but complex edges around the box.

Although we only lightly touched on it, we have learned how to make a whole layer transparent when the player is overlapping an object. This can be used in all kinds of games, such as 2D RPG games, where walking into a building reveals what is under the roof.

Have a go hero – design a custom panel image

In the **Layout Editor**, try changing the Image of the Panel object to a more complex image with thicker borders (defined in the Properties box as the image margins).

Pop quiz – recap

Now that our game is playable, lets take a quick look back at some knowledge we've gained through a multiple choice pop quiz.

1. What `Platform` behavior action can we use to stop the player from moving?

    a. Set ignoring input

    b. Set activated

    c. Stop

2. Why do we use the overlapping condition instead of an `On collision` condition for setting the player animation to `"Win"`?

    a. To prevent the player from reverting to default animations

    b. To ensure the player wins every time they touch the post

    c. `On collision` will only trigger when a collision action is used

3. When do bad guys change their direction?

    a. When they are not facing the player

    b. When they collide with spikes

    c. When they collide with the level walls

Summary

This chapter really picked up the pace from the last one, and as such we covered a lot of territory. We first learned how to code a goal post to end the game in victory for the player, before moving on to make obstacles that take away the player's life on contact.

Following that, we added a death and life system to allow the player more tries at winning, but also learned how to move enemies using events and give the player a way to beat them to add a further challenge. We finally learned how panel objects can make a HUD more interesting and easy to use

Right now, we can make a playable game, but it feels empty without any sound or music playing. Luckily, that is the topic of the next chapter.

4
Making Noise

In the previous chapter, we finished making our game playable and challenging. However, we have no easy way to give feedback to the player. This is where sounds and music save the day.

In this chapter, we shall:

◆ Learn how to add looping music to our game

◆ Learn how the Mod plugin works and why it is useful

◆ Use sounds to make our game more immersive

◆ Learn how to export our game to share with friends

So let's get on with it.

A game and its music

A game can be made more interesting or emotional through music. It can have specially made music (such as the original Mario Bros theme song), or even introduce a music piece to a wider audience (such as the song used in Tetris).

Music is described as *looping* when it repeats constantly. Looped music is great for games as it always plays continuously, regardless of how long the player takes to beat a level.

Time for action – add some music to our game

Our player doesn't have anything to listen to while playing our game. We're going to change that by adding a looped MP3 music file to the game.

1. Find a song file of the MP3 format (.mp3) that you would like to play in the background of your game.

2. Rename this file to Game.mp3 (or simply Game if you do not have file extensions visible).

3. Put the renamed song file in the same folder as our game project, and then open up the game in Construct Classic.

4. In the **Layout Editor**, select the layer **Game** and then insert a new object into the layout.

5. Choose the object **XAudio2** from the object group **Audio** and click on **Insert**.

6. Now switch over to the **Event Sheet Editor** and insert a new event. Choose the highlighted event **Start of layout** from the System object and click on **Finish**.

7. Add an action for this event and choose the **XAudio2** object. Select the highlighted action **Play music from file** and click on **Next**.

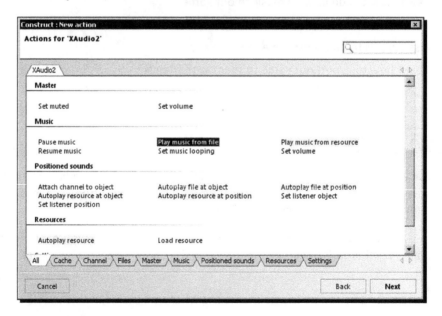

8. In the next screen, enter the text `AppPath & "Game.mp3"` and click on **Finish**.

9. To get the music to loop, add another action for the `XAudio2` object and select the action **Set music looping** before clicking on **Next**.

10. Finally, choose the option **Loop** from the drop-down box and click on **Finish**.

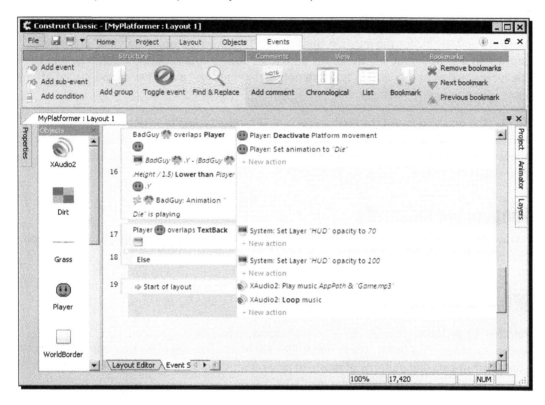

What just happened?

We now have music playing in the background of our game that will loop forever. Let's see how we did it.

The start of layout condition

To load and play the music when the level starts, we use the start of a layout condition to play the music. This is triggered wherever the layout is transitioned to as well (so that the music will restart when the player's character dies).

Playing the music file

We used an MP3 file for the music in this project. The XAudio2 object can also play WMA music files and would require the music path AppPath & "Game.wma" instead (where the file is renamed to Game.wma). It is worth noting that only one music file can be played at once from the XAudio2 object.

To play the music, we used the term AppPath. This references the folder where the game is run from, and hence we just need to look for the filename of our song, rather than writing the whole directory for it. We can also put our music file in the folder Music and then reference the file as AppPath & "\Music\" & "Game.mp3".

Looping the music file

To loop the music, we added an action to tell it to. This same action can also be used to stop the music from looping.

Modules of music

Another music format that can be used is the module format range (.xm, .it, .mod, .s3m, and many other extensions). These music files are of much smaller size than MP3s as they store instruments and patterns of music to play rather than continuous sound wave data. This makes them great for video games.

Although we already have music in our game, we'll take a look at how we could have added module music to our game in order to know how to do it in future games.

Time for action – play some mod music

It's always good to know alternate ways of doing things, and so we are going to learn to how to play module files—another type of file that can contain music.

1. Start a new blank game project in Construct and name it ModTest.

2. Insert the MOD object into the layout from the group **Audio**.

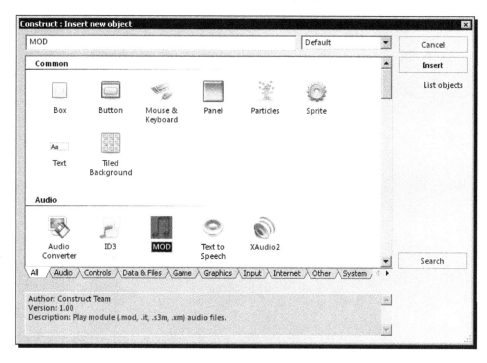

3. Save the project in a folder of your choice, and then find a module file of .xm or .it format. These can be found online and are often free to download (a further benefit of using them in games).

4. Put this music file in the same folder as the project and return to Construct Classic.

5. Now switch to the **Event Sheet Editor**.

6. Insert a new event and choose the MOD object. Then select the condition **Is Playing** and then **invert** it.

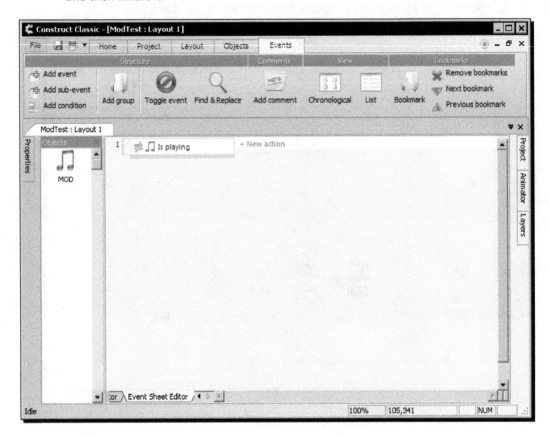

7. Now, add a new action for the event, choose the MOD object again, and select the action **Load file**.

8. In the next box, enter AppPath & "Yoursong.ext", where Yoursong is the name of your chosen song file and .ext is the extension of your song (.xm or .it).

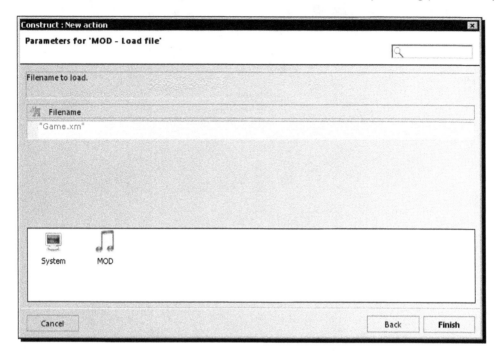

9. Add another action from the MOD object, this time selecting **Play**, as in the following screenshot:

10. Now run the game to test that the song both plays and loops.

What just happened?

We've now just set up the same thing we had earlier, but with module music files instead. Although the tutorial suggested using a .xm or .it format, any module format should work with the object. However, let's look at what is different about this object.

The Is playing condition

A handy condition of the MOD object is the Is playing condition. This triggers whenever the music is still playing, and hence we invert it to check when the music is stopped. We use this to restart the music when it is finished.

Loading and playing the file

With this object, we need to load the song file we want to play into memory before playing it. This is done in a single action for the XAudio2 object.

Sounds: describing the action

Sounds are used in games to give the player feedback on what is going on. Whether they are taking damage or jumping, the player uses sounds to have further insight on what is happening in the game.

Sound effects can also make it easier to time jumps and motions in games, which is useful for our game. Now let's see how to add them.

Time for action – adding sounds

After our short break away from it, we return to put the final ingredient in our platformer: sound.

1. Record or find sound effects for, the actions jumping, dying, winning, and hitting an enemy. Name these sound effects Jump.wav, Die.wav, Win.wav, and Hit.wav accordingly. A useful free tool for recording retro sound effects is SFXR.

2. Copy these sound effects to the project folder and open MyPlatformer up again, entering the **Event Sheet Editor**.

3. To start, we'll play a sound whenever the player jumps. Add a new event to the event sheet. Select the Player object and from the **Platform** tab, choose the condition **Is jumping** and click on **Finish**. Then complete the event with a Trigger once while true condition.

4. Now add an action for this event from the XAudio2 object. Select the highlighted action Autoplay file and click on Next. Enter the text AppPath & "Jump. wav", and click on **Finish** to see a display similar to the following screenshot:

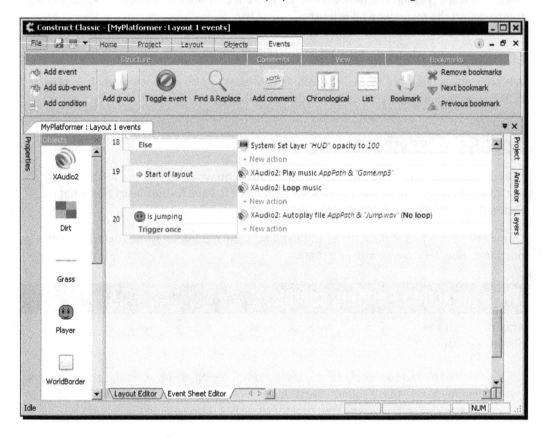

5. Next, add another event for the Player object with the conditions **Animation "Die" is playing** and **Trigger once while true**.

6. Give this event an `Autoplay file` action as well, with the sound `Die.wav` instead, as in the following screenshot:

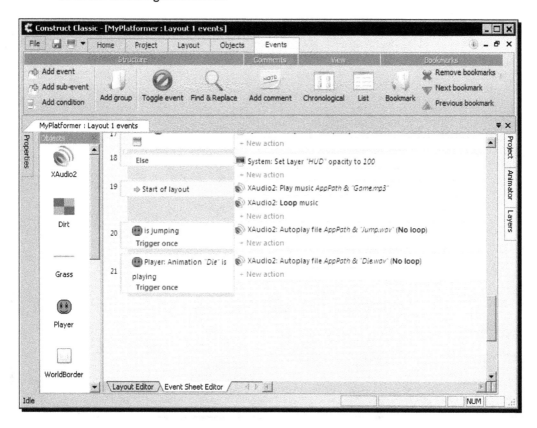

7. Now add another event for when the animation `Win` is playing. Change the sound filename to `Win.wav`.

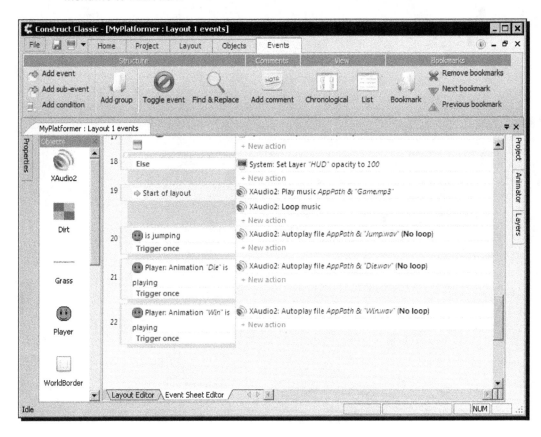

8. Finally, scroll up to the event where the player hits an enemy on the head and bounces, and add an action to play the sound `Hit.wav`, as shown in the following screenshot:

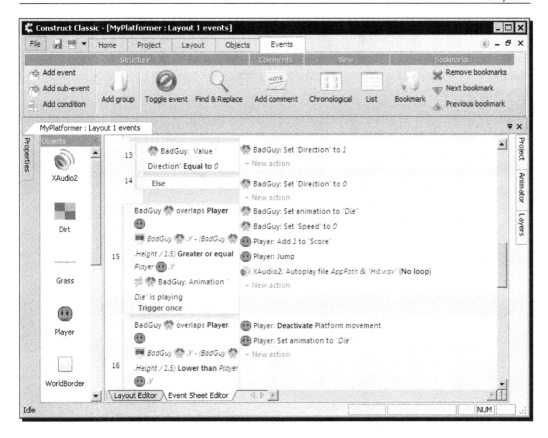

What just happened?

We now have sounds that play in our game to tell the player a bit more about what is going on. By using the `Autoplay file` action, we simply feed a sound file and tell it whether or not to loop the sound.

Exporting our game

Before we can share our finished game with others, we need to export it. This is where the project file is turned into an executable program so that people can play it without Construct Classic.

Once we export our game, we only need to include the executable, sound, and music files it uses to send to others.

Time for action – exporting our game

In these next steps, we'll be making our project playable on other computers that don't have Construct installed. This is important to ensure everyone can play our game.

1. In Construct, open the **Project** ribbon tab at the top of the screen, as in the following screenshot:

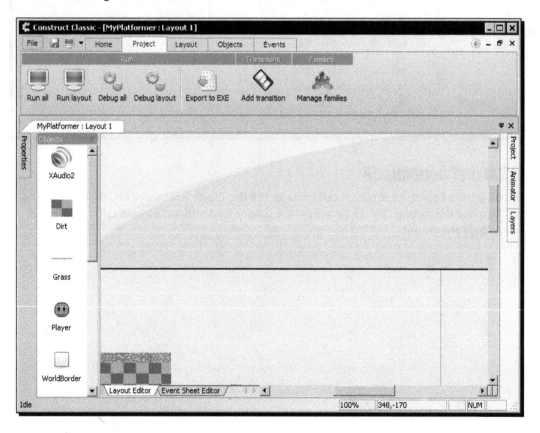

2. Click on the button that says **Export to EXE**. You will see the following screen. We do not need to check the **Enable python** option, as we did not use any Python scripting in our game. In most cases, we will never need to use Python in our games.

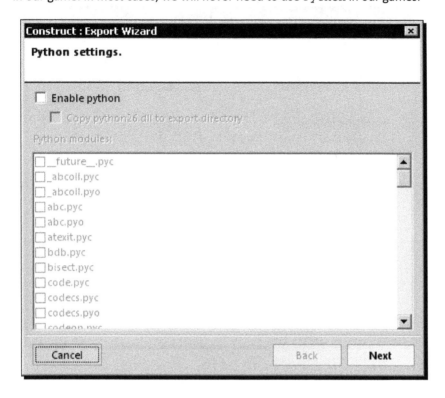

3. Click on **Next** to skip the screen, and we will now see the options shown in the following screenshot:

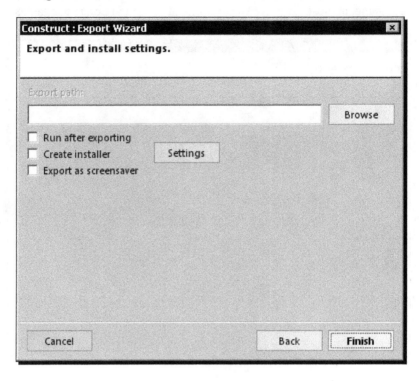

4. Click **Browse** to choose the folder you would like to export the program to. Create a brand new folder named Game, and then enter it before entering the filename MyPlatformer and clicking **Save**.

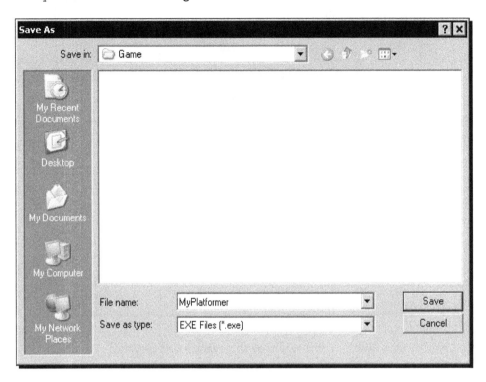

5. Now we return to the following screen. Click on **Finish** to export the game.

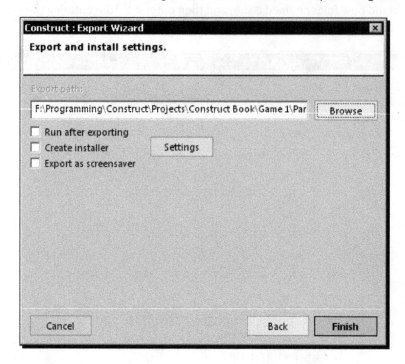

6. We then see an export bar similar to the following screenshot:

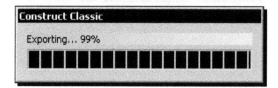

7. Wait for the bar to disappear, and then open the folder where the game was exported and copy all of the sound and music files to the folder.

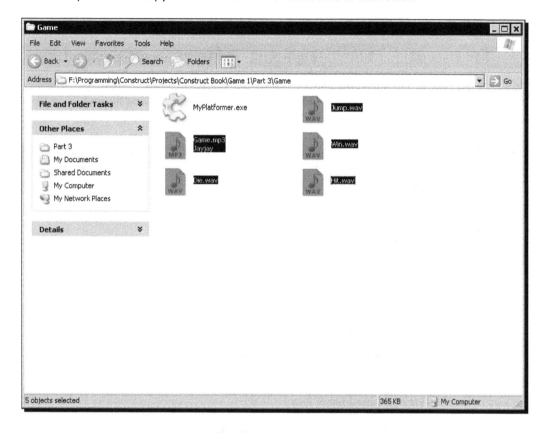

8. This folder is now ready to be copied to other computers, or zipped and shared online. To zip the folder, right-click on it and select **Send To | Compressed (zipped) Folder** from the context menu.

9. When trying to run the program, simply double-click on MyPlatformer.exe.

What just happened?

We have now finished our first full game and have it ready to distribute. Follow these steps each time you export a game.

Have a go hero – make another platformer

Now that we have finished our first game in Construct Classic, take the knowledge we've gained and try making another platformer. This time, try adding a moving floor (in the same way we moved the enemies back and forth) and using module music files.

Pop quiz – sound and music

Let's try a multiple choice pop quiz to see how much we remember of the chapter.

1. What is true about differences between MOD and MP3 files?

    a. MOD files are usually smaller in file size

    b. MOD music files can have different file extensions

    c. MP3 files can be played with the XAudio2 plugin

    d. All of the above

2. What condition and action(s) set do we use to loop a MOD file?

    a. Start of layout – play music from file

    b. Is Playing – play music from resource

    c. Is Playing – load file & Play

3. What do we distribute when our game is exported for others to play it?

    a. The source cap, sound, and music files

    b. The executable, sound, and music files

    c. All files we used to make the game

A note on sharing our games

Before we finish this chapter, it is worth noting that any game made in Construct Classic can be given away, or sold, without any payment due to the developers of the editor. There are no hidden clauses in the license that give them ownership of your work and no requirements to mention that your game was made in Construct Classic. However, this does not extend to the media we use. If we use any media files that we do not own, then we must have permission or a license from the original author to do so.

Summary

We now know how to put sounds and music into our games. This was an important step as we'll be using it throughout the next games we will be making together. You'll be using this knowledge in most games you make after you finish the book, as well as the knowledge of exporting your finished executable.

Our main point of learning was how to add MP3 music to our game using XAudio2 or its alternative module music formats using the MOD object. We then learned how to play sounds from our game folder and finally to package our game into an executable program to share with others.

We also discussed how games we make with Construct Classic can be freely sold or given away without any licensing issues, provided that we have ownership or permission to use the media files in the game.

Now that we've learned the basics of making a platform game in Construct Classic, we're ready to learn how to use the built-in physics engine Box2D to make a puzzle game, which we're starting in the next chapter.

5
Practical Physics

For our second creation, we're going to make a casual puzzle game similar to PopCap's Peggle and Japanese casino game Pachinko. In this game, we will fire a ball from a launcher towards the mouse and it will bounce off pegs, which then disappear, as it falls off the screen. We will also have certain pegs that must be hit to clear the level and special portals to teleport the ball to another position. We'll do this using Box2D, the physics engine implemented in Construct Classic.

In this chapter, we shall:

- Learn how to use the Physics behavior to make objects that move realistically
- Learn about event sheets, groups, and how they make game development easier
- Learn how to add forces to the ball as it hits a peg or is launched
- Add specialty pegs to our game
- Create portals to tunnel the ball to another position
- Use particles to create fireworks when a level is finished
- Add sound effects and music into our game
- Create and transition to new layouts upon level completion
- Learn how to use the debugger

So let's get on with it.

Creating physical objects

The **Physics** behavior is used whenever an object is needed to interact or behave with realistic motion. It is also needed for other objects with the behavior to collide properly, meaning most objects in our game are going to need the behavior.

Time for action – creating our objects

For our game, we need to have our objects in the layout before we can create events for them. Let's make them now.

1. We'll need to draw up some graphics for the objects of our game. A name and example for each of the objects we need are shown in the following figure:

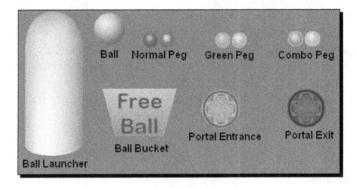

2. Now draw a background of size 800x600 for the first level, as in the following screenshot:

3. Next, open Construct and click on the Project Properties to change the **Name** to `BounceBall`, and enter your name as the `Creator`. Also, scroll down in the properties box to set the **Window Width** to `800` and **Window Height** to `600`.

4. Then create three layers in the first layout: `HUD`, `Objects`, and `Background` (with `HUD` being the topmost layer and `Background` being the lowest).

5. On the background layer, create the sprite `BackgroundImg1` and paste your background image. Set the hotspot to the top-left corner of the image and its position to `0` for **X** and `0` for **Y**. Stretch the background to the size of the layout and then lock the layer.

6. Now, in the **Objects** layer create the sprites `BallLauncher`, `Ball`, `Bucket`, and `Portal`. Centre the hotspot (*numpad 5*) for all except the `BallLauncher` and `Bucket`. The hotspots for these are shown in the following screenshot:

7. For the `BallLauncher` object, click on the blue **Image points** tool and click on the + box in the tool options to `Remove` the current image point `point`.

8. Type `1` in the box and click on **Add** before clicking on **Close**. Then, place the point at the end of the launcher barrel. We'll use this point as the position the ball will be launched from.

9. Create a new sprite on the **Objects** layer for the `Peg` object. This object will have the animations `Normal`, `NormalHit`, `Green`, `GreenHit`, `Combo`, and `ComboHit`. Examples of `Normal` and `NormalHit` is shown in the following screenshot:

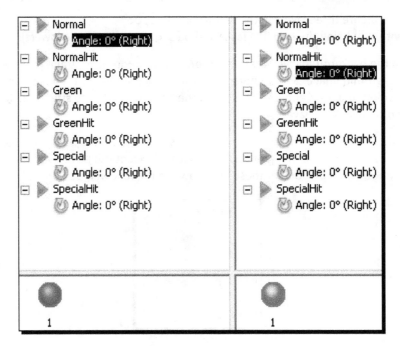

10. Set the size of the `Peg` object on the layout to `20` by `20` and the size of the ball object to `12` by `12`. For the `Portal` objects, use the size `40` by `40`.

11. Create the `XAudio2` and `Mouse & Keyboard` objects in the same layer, and in their properties check the box **Global**. We now have the objects as in the following screenshot:

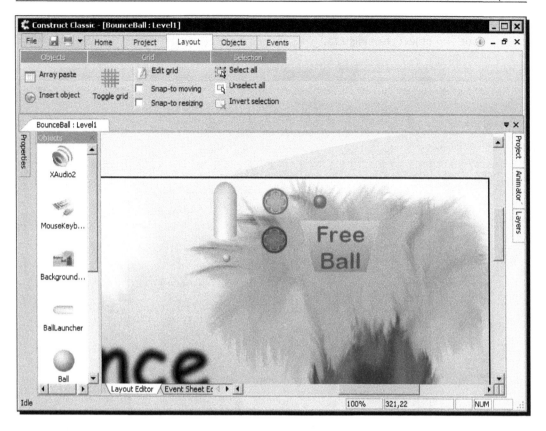

12. Set the **X** position of the `BallLauncher` and `Bucket` objects to `400` (midway along the layout) and the **Y** position of both a small distance from the edges.

13. Now, in the **Layout** ribbon menu option, click on the button **Edit Grid** and set the grid size to `34` by `34`, as in the following screenshot:

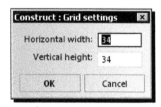

14. Check the box **Snap-to moving** and click on **Toggle Grid**. We now have a grid that our `Peg` objects can align to.

15. Copy-and-paste the `Peg` object to make a level.

16. Position the portal objects around the level as well. An example of a completed level design is shown in the following screenshot:

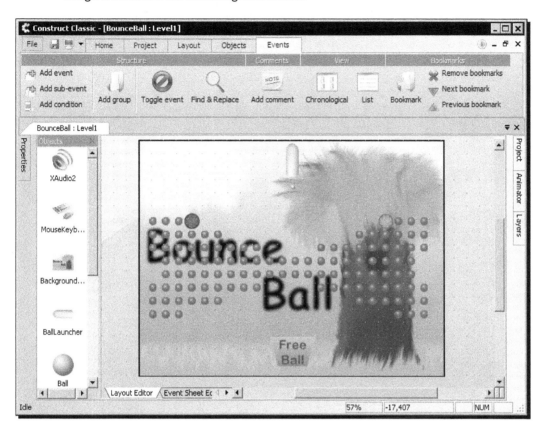

17. Now we need a sprite for the lip of the bucket, which will be used to *catch* the ball. Create a black sprite `BucketCatch` with a centered hotspot and position it as shown in the following screenshot (uncheck **Snap-to moving** and hide the grid again):

18. Record the difference in height between the `Bucket` and `BucketCatch` objects. This is done by writing down what remains when the **Y** position of `BucketCatch` is subtracted from the **Y** position of `Bucket`. We can store the information in a `Text` object outside the layout without any effect on our game, but we can delete it when we finish the game. This will be used later for keeping the `BucketCatch` object *attached* while the `Bucket` object is moving.

19. We now have our objects ready for behaviors to be added to them. Select the `Ball` object and add the behavior `Physics`.

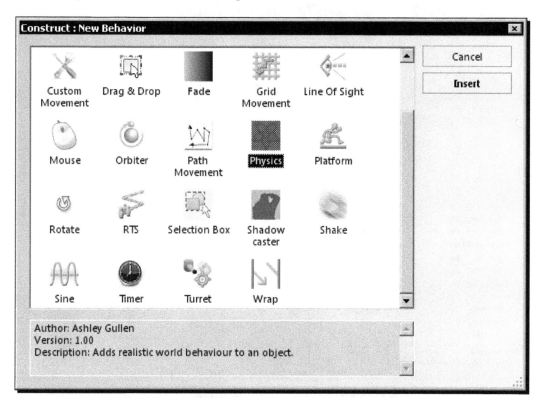

20. For the `Physics` behavior, check **Gravity** and **No Rotation** before setting **Mass** to 2 and setting the values **Linear damping**, **Angular damping**, and **Contact friction** to 0%.

21. Next, set **Contact elasticity** to 80% and **Collision mask** to **Ellipse**.

22. Now ensure that **Simulation Steps** is set to 10 and **World X scale** and **World Y scale** are both set to 2%, and finally that **World Gravity** is set to 7. We will not need to change these last values in future as they are global to all `Physics` behaviors.

23. The properties of the physics behavior should match the following screenshot:

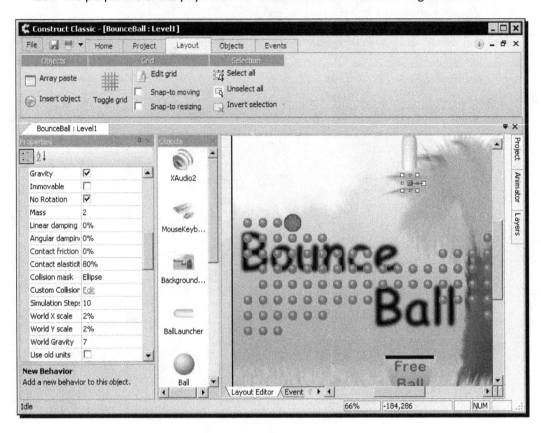

24. In the **Objects** bar, click on the **Peg** object to select all of them and then add the `Physics` behavior. Use the settings as in the following screenshot:

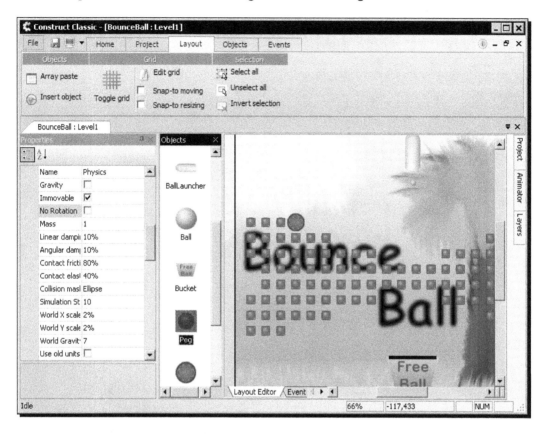

25. Add the `Timer` behavior to the `Peg` objects as well.

26. Next, add the `Physics` behavior to the `Bucket` object and choose the **Collision mask** option **Custom**. Then, click on `Edit` in the box underneath, and left-click on place points around the outline of the `Bucket` object.

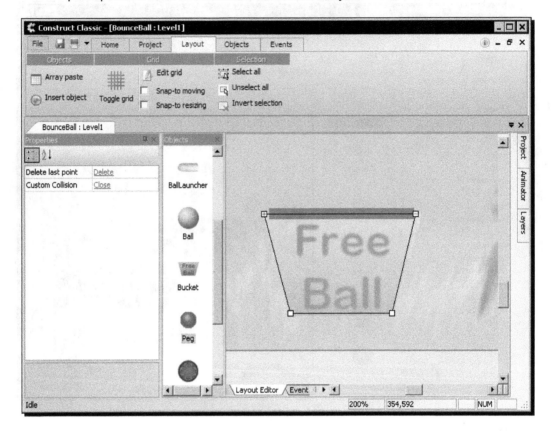

27. For this object, check only **No Rotation** and set the **Mass** to `4000`; everything else can be left the same as its default value.

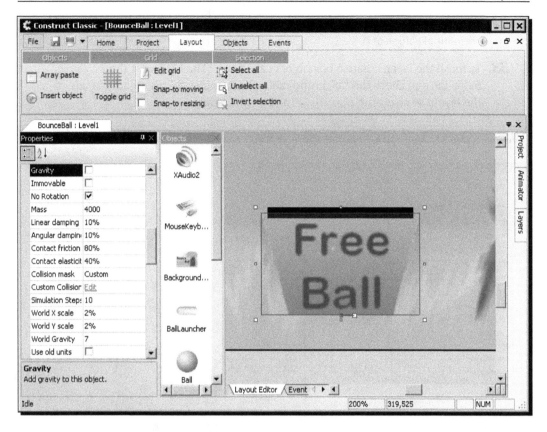

28. We can now add our global and private variables to the game. Start by creating the global variables `GreenLeft`, `ShotScore`, and `TotalScore` with initial values of `0`.

29. Create a private variable for the `Peg` objects (to select them all, click their image from the `Objects` bar) named `Hit` with a value of `0`.

30. Select the `BallLauncher` object and give it the private variables `BallsLeft`, `CanShoot`, `ComboActivated`, and `NumCombo`. Set all initial values to `0` apart from `BallsLeft`, which has an initial value of `10`.

31. Then, select the `Bucket` object and give it the private variable `Direction` with value `1`.

32. The `Ball` object will also need the private variables `VelocityX` and `VelocityY` with initial values of `0`.

33. To finish the layer, create a box object called `LevelWall`, give it the `Physics` behavior, and check the box **Immovable**. Place copies of this object outside of the layout to cover the `top`, `left`, and `right` sides.

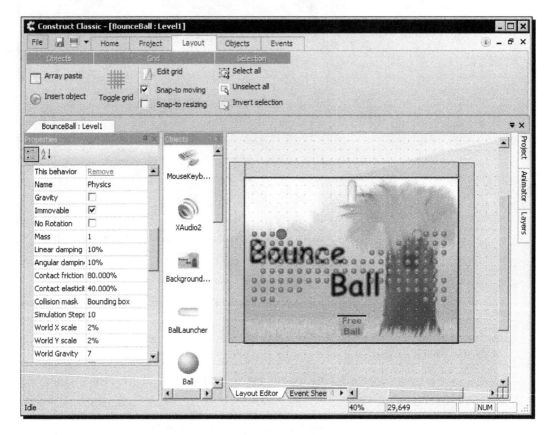

34. We can now add the final objects we'll need—the HUD texts. Select the HUD layer and create the text objects `txtBallsLeft`, `txtGreens`, `txtMessage`, `txtTotal`, and `txtShot`. Choose an easily visible font color and size so the text objects are visible over our level image, and use a slightly brighter color for the `txtMessage` object.

35. Set the `Horizontal alignment` property of the `txtTotal` and `txtShot` to `Right`. Then set the `Text` property to `Total Score: 0` for `txtTotal` and `Shot Score: 0` for `txtShot`.

36. Now, set the `Text` properties of `txtBallsLeft`, `txtGreens`, and `txtMessage` to `Balls Left: 10`, `Green Pegs Left: 12`, and `Click to launch ball` respectively.

37. Finally, position these three text objects on the left as shown in the following screenshot:

What just happened?

We have now created all of the sprites and text objects we will be using to make our game. We did this using the previous knowledge from making our first game. However, we also expanded on this by giving some objects the Physics behavior.

Let's take a closer look at what we did while creating the objects.

The Global property

For the `XAudio2` and `Mouse & Keyboard` object, we gave them the `Global` property. This causes them to be created in all layouts automatically. We'll be using them later in this chapter when we learn to create and change to additional levels.

Aligning to a grid

We learned how to view and edit the size of the grid. We also learned that the **Snap-to moving** box allowed us to move objects according to the grid points; this was used to position our pegs. The additional option **Snap-to resizing** forces the objects to fit the grid squares during resizing.

Setting the Physics properties

When we added the Physics behavior to our objects, we needed to set the properties of the behavior for each object. We started with the ball and gave it the ability to be affected by gravity, but not rotate while moving. The ball also used the Collision mask setting Ellipse, which represents either a circle or oval.

We gave the ball a frictionless movement through air by setting the damping and friction forces to 0%. However, we used a Contact elasticity of 80% to slow our ball down as it collides with objects. This elasticity affects how fast the ball remains after hitting an object (in this case, 80 percent of its speed before colliding).

The other property we used, besides Gravity and No Rotation, was Immovable. This prevents the object from moving at all when hit or commanded to through events.

The Timer behavior

For our Peg objects, we also attached the Timer behavior to it. This behavior adds events that can start unique timers on its object and perform actions when they are finished. We'll be using this to destroy our Peg objects a few seconds after the ball first hits them.

Creating a custom physics collision mask

For our Bucket object, the Bounding Box and Ellipse collision masks did not accurately represent its shape. We then had to use a Custom collision mask and draw the outline of the object. This collision mask allows for complex shapes, but will slow down a game when too many are used.

Event sheets and groups

If we wanted to make a different level for our platformer game, we would need to copy-and-paste all of the events into the new layout. With **Event sheets**, the same events can be re-used across many different layouts. This is also useful for separating different sheets of events, as more than one event sheet can be imported in a single layout.

Inside an event sheet, we can also use **Groups**. These are able to separate events and can also be activated, or deactivated, with actions. As with the importing of event sheets, many groups can exist in a single event sheet.

Time for action – creating and using Event sheets and groups

Before we create our game events, we'll need an event sheet to include in each of the levels of our game. We'll also need groups to separate the events into understandable sections.

1. Open the **Project** view and rename our first layout to Level1 and its event sheet to Level1 events.

2. Then, right-click the folder Event Sheets, then click the option Add event sheet.

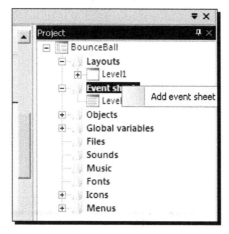

3. Click on the new event sheet name to rename it to Game. Then switch over to the **Event Sheet Editor** in our Level1 layout.

4. Right-click on this layout to bring up the context menu and select **Include event sheet**. We then have a white bar we can right-click to select the Game event sheet.

5. Next, right-click on the white bar again and select **Go-to include** to open the Game event sheet in a new tab.

6. We now have our event sheet ready for groups to be added to it. Right-click the empty space and select **Insert group** from the context menu. Enter a **Title** of the **Game** and description of **Main game code**.

7. To finish, create our second group HUD with the description `Code for the heads up display` as in the following screenshot:

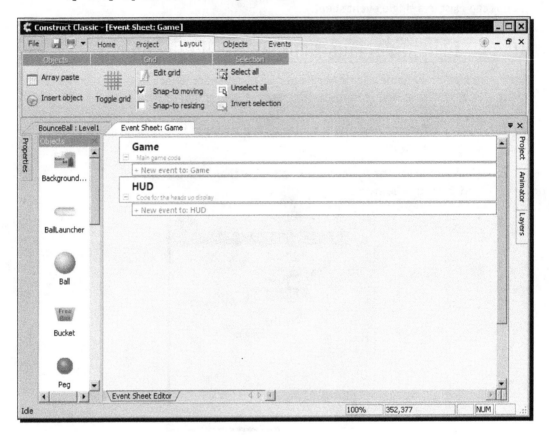

What just happened?

We now have our groups and event sheet ready for coding our game. This was a short process but will help the organization of our events.

Adding a physical force

The Physics behavior can automatically apply a force of gravity to objects and forces of collision between objects. To exert external forces, such as ball launch and the repulsion of a peg when first hit, we need to use events.

Time for action – creating forces

If we just let the ball drop straight down, the game would become very boring and not all green pegs would be hit. We are therefore going to set up the ball launcher, peg, bucket movements, and forces. We'll also create some basic game structure events.

1. To start, create an `Always` event in the `Game` group. The first action for this will be for the `BucketCatch` object and is called `Set position`.

2. Enter the **X** and **Y** of `Bucket.X` and `Bucket.Y - 73` (otherwise known as the distance between them, as we measured in the last topic).

3. Add the action for rotating the ball launcher to the mouse within the angle range of `10` and `170` degrees. Choose the action **Set angle** for the `BallLauncher` object and enter `Clamp(Angle(BallLauncher.X, BallLauncher.Y, MouseX, MouseY), 10, 170)` as the text.

4. Add an action for the `Physics` behavior of the `Bucket` object. Choose **Set velocity** and enter `Bucket.Value('Direction') * 3` as the **X component** and `0` as the **Y component**. This will cause the bucket to move in its direction.

5. Now we can add our depth actions to order which sprites appear in front of each other. Create a `Send to front` action for each of these objects in the order `PortalOut`, `PortalIn`, `Ball`, `Bucket`, `Peg`, and finally `BallLauncher`.

6. Next, we'll add a new event in the Game group. Select the BallLauncher object and the highlighted condition Compare a private variable, and compare the variable CanShoot to being Greater than the number 0.

7. Right-click on this event and choose **Insert sub-event** from the context menu with the MouseKeyboard condition On click. Choose the **Mouse button** option **Left**.

8. Give this sub-event the action Create object at image point from the System actions and select the Ball object for the first box. Then enter "Objects" as the layer to create on, and set the **Object to position to** as the BallLauncher object at image point 1.

9. Add another action for the BallLauncher object named Subtract from value to remove 1 from the variable BallsLeft.

10. Add an action for the Physics behavior of the Ball object of name Add force towards position. Set the **X co-ordinate** to BallLauncher.X, the **Y co-ordinate** to BallLauncher.Y, and the **Force** to -50. This will launch the ball away from the BallLauncher object.

11. To finish the sub-event, create an action for the BallLauncher of name Set value to set the value of **CanShoot** to 0.

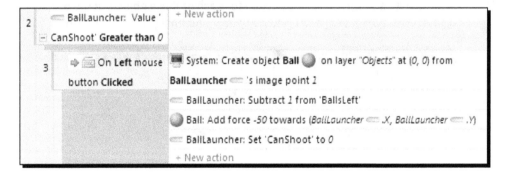

12. Now add a new event to the Game group with the highlighted condition **On collision with another object** for the Ball object. Choose the object Peg and click on **Finish**.

13. Next, add another condition to the event. Choose the highlighted condition **Compare a private variable** for the Peg object and compare Hit to see if it is equal to 0.

14. Add the action Set animation for the Peg object and choose the animation Peg. AnimName & :"Hit".

15. Add another action to the event for the Peg object, selecting the Timer action Start timer. Enter a **Timer name** of "TimeOut" and **Timer length** of 5000 - random(2000). To finish the action, set the **Destroy** box to Destroy.

16. Now add an action for the `Physics` behavior of the `Ball` object. Choose **Add force** to position the action and enter an **X co-ordinate** of `Peg.X`, **Y co-ordinate** of `Peg.Y`, and **Force** of `-0.5 * (sqrt(Ball[Physics].VelocityX ^ 2 + Ball[Physics].VelocityY ^ 2))`. This will repel the ball from the peg with force relative to its contact speed.

17. Create a `Set value` action for the `Peg` object to set `Hit` to 1.

18. Add a sub-event to this event now with the condition `An animation is playing` for the `Peg` object, checking to see if the animation is `"NormalHit"`.

19. Give this sub-event the `System` action **Add to value** to add `100 + (BallLauncher.Value('ComboActivated') * 100)` to **ShotScore**.

20. Add another event to the `Game` group. Choose the condition **Object is outside layout?** for the `Ball` object and click on **Finish**.

21. Create the action `Destroy` for the `Ball` object to finish this event.

22. Create a new event again for the `Ball` object, this time choosing the condition **Is overlapping another object**. Choose the object `BallCatch` and click on **Finish**.

23. Add the action `Add to value` for the `BallLauncher` object to add 1 to `BallsLeft`.

24. Add the final action `Destroy` to the event for the `Ball` object.

25. Now, create yet another event for the `Game` group, this time with the `Bucket` object and highlighted condition **On collision with another object**. Choose the object `LevelWall` and click on **Finish**.

26. Insert another condition to the event, this time choosing **Trigger once while true** from the `System` object, and click on **Finish**.

27. Add an action to the event for the `Bucket`. Choose **Set value** and use it to set the value of **Direction** to `Bucket.Value('Direction') * -1`. This will flip the direction the bucket moves in.

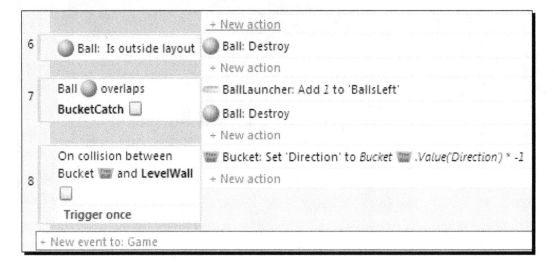

28. Create another event in the `Game` group with the highlighted `System` condition `Compare` to compare if `Ball.Count` is `Lower or equal` to 0.

29. Add the highlighted condition **Compare a private variable** for the `BallLauncher` object to check if `BallsLeft` is `Greater than` the value 0.

30. Add the same condition again for the `BallLauncher` object, but checking if **CanShoot** is `Equal` to the value 0.

31. Insert the highlighted action **Set value** for the `BallLauncher` object twice to set **CanShoot** to 1 and **ComboActivated** to 0.

32. Then insert the `Add to value` action for the `System` object. Choose to add `global('ShotScore')` to **TotalScore**.

33. To finish the event, add the highlighted action `Set value` to set **ShotScore** to 0.

34. Make a new event for the `Peg` object of highlighted condition **Compare a private variable** to check if **Hit is Equal** to the value 1.

35. Give this event the highlighted action **Set value** for the `BallLauncher` to set the value of **CanShoot** to 0.

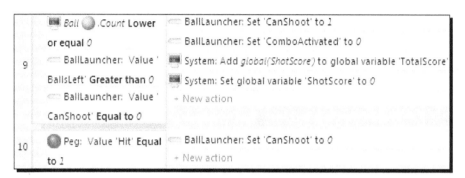

36. To finish, create an `Always` event from the `System` object in the HUD group.

37. Insert the highlighted **Set text** action for `txtBallsLeft` and enter a text of `"Balls Left: " & BallLauncher.Value('BallsLeft')`.

38. Then insert the same action again for `txtGreens`, this time with text `"Green Pegs Left: " & global('GreenLeft')`.

39. Use another action to set the text of `txtShot` to `"Shot Score: " & global('ShotScore')`.

40. Finally, set the text of **txtTotal** to `"Total Score: " & global('TotalScore')`.

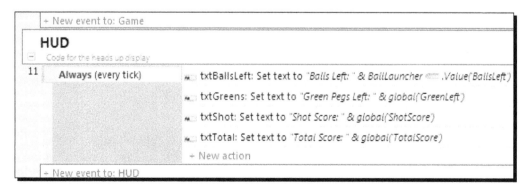

What just happened?

We've now created the events that form the backbone of our game. We have events to handle the launch of a ball, the catch of a ball, the movement of the bucket, and the bouncing off a peg that hasn't been hit yet. In our `Always` event, we also used `Send to front` actions to order sprites that will be in front of others.

It is worth noting the use of the Clamp expression. This is used to lock a value within a minimum and a maximum range. We used this to ensure the `BallLauncher` object does not rotate backwards/upside down.

Adding special pegs

Our game is playable, but we'll want to have a goal to win and bonus for skilled players. This is where special pegs come in. We'll be using green pegs to represent the pegs that must be hit to clear a level and a blue peg to start a 2x combo when hit. The green pegs are randomly selected from the normal pegs on the level start, while a blue peg is randomly chosen from normal pegs at the end of each shot.

Time for action – creating specialty pegs

Our player will want a method to win the level, as well as a method of getting a higher score through some carefully planned shots. This is where the green and blue pegs come in to play.

1. In the `Game` group, create a new event with the `System` highlighted condition **Start of layout** and drag it to the top of the list of events.

2. Insert the `Set visible` action for the `BucketCatch` object and select `Invisible` before clicking on **Finish**.

3. Add two highlighted `Set value` actions for the `System` object. For the first, set the value of **GreenLeft** to `12`, and for the second, set the value of **ShotScore** to `0`.

4. Right-click on the event and select **Insert sub-event** from the context menu. Choose the `System` condition **For**. Enter the **Name** as `"FillGreen"`, **Start** as `1`, and **End** as `global('GreenLeft')`. Click on **Finish**.

5. Give this event a sub-event of its own. Choose the condition **An animation is playing** for the `Peg` object and enter the animation name `"Normal"` before clicking on **Finish**.

6. Add a new condition for this sub-event. Selecting the `Peg` object again, choose the condition **Pick a random object** and finish the condition.

7. Create the action `Set animation` for the `Peg` object and enter the animation `"Green"` before finishing the action.

8. Right-click on the `Start of layout` event again to insert a new sub-event, and give it the same conditions as steps 5 and 6.

9. Give this event the action `Set animation` for the `Peg` object and enter the animation name `"Special"`.

10. Add another action to the event. This time, choose the highlighted action `Set value` for the `BallLauncher` object and set the value of **NumCombo** to 1.

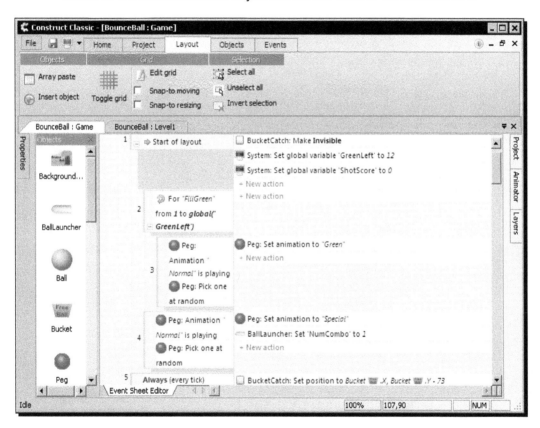

11. Now scroll down to the event `On collision between Ball and Peg`. Insert a new sub-event checking to see if the animation of the `Peg` is `"GreenHit"`.

12. For this event, use the `Subtract from value` action from the `System` object to remove 1 from the value of **GreenLeft**.

13. Insert an `Add to value` action from the `System` object and add `150 +`
`(BallLauncher.Value('ComboActivated') * 150)` to **ShotScore**.

14. Insert another sub-event for the parent event to check whether the `Peg` animation
is instead `"Special"`.

15. Give this event the highlighted action **Set value** for the object `BallLauncher`
and set the value of **ComboActivated** to `1`.

16. Create a second **Set value** action for the `BallLauncher` object to set
NumCombo to `0`.

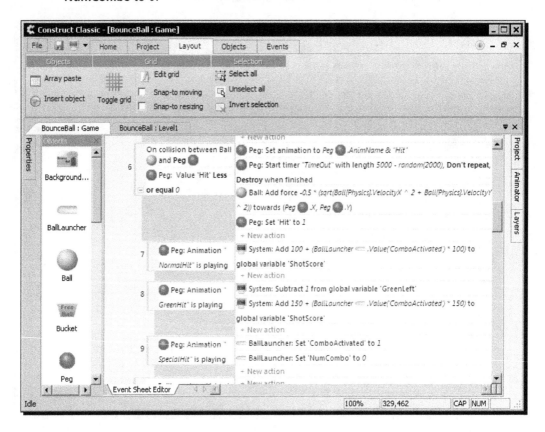

17. Scroll to the next main event, `BallLauncher Value 'CanShoot' Greater`
`than 0`, and create a new sub-event to check whether the `Peg` animation
`"Normal"` is playing. Drag this sub-event above the existing **On Left mouse
button Clicked** sub-event.

18. Give this new sub-event the condition **Pick an object at random** for the `Peg` object, as well as another condition to check if the private variable `"NumCombo"` of the `BallLauncher` object is equal to `0`.

19. Create an action to set the animation of the `Peg` object to `"Special"` and a second action to set the value of `"NumCombo"` for the `BallLauncher` object to `1`.

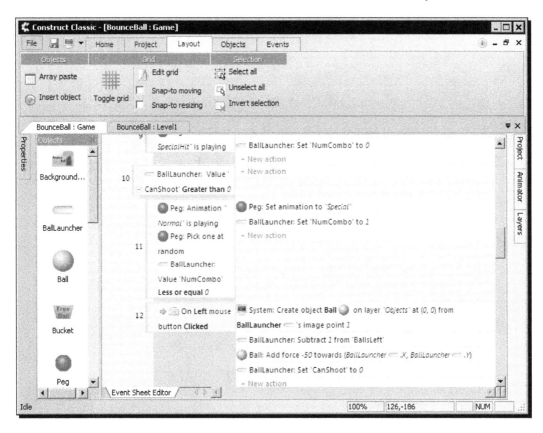

20. Now scroll down to the event `Ball.Count Lower or equal 0` and create a sub-event for it. Use this sub-event to check if the animation `"Special"` is playing for the `Peg` object.

21. Create an action to set this `Peg` object animation to `"Normal"` and a second action to set the private variable `"NumCombo"` to `0` for the `BallLauncher` action.

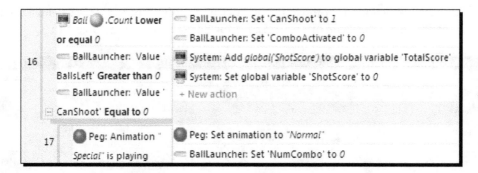

22. Create a new event at the bottom of the `Game` for the `MouseKeyboard` object and select the condition `Mouse button is down?`. Choose the mouse button `Right` and click on **Finish**.

23. Create an additional condition for this event to check if `Ball.Count` is lower or equal to `0`.

24. Give this event the action **Set time scale** from the `System` object and enter the value `4` before clicking on **Finish**. This will speed up time while the right button of the mouse is held down.

25. Create another event following this and give it the `System` object condition `Else`. This will activate when the previous event does not trigger. Note that the `Else` event is now attached to the previous event.

26. Insert an action for this `Else` event to set the time scale back to `1`, as in the following screenshot. This will return the game to normal speed when the right button of the mouse is released or a ball has been fired.

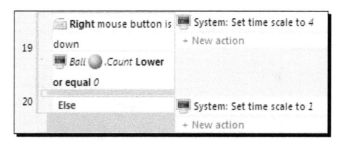

27. Now insert an event in the HUD group to check if the `BallLauncher` variable `"CanShoot"` is equal to `1`.

28. Use the `Set text` action of the `txtMessage` object to set its text to `"Click to launch ball"`.

29. Add the action `Set visible` to make the `txtMessage` object `Visible`.

30. Create another event for the `HUD` group, this time checking if the `BallLauncher` variable `"CanShoot"` is equal to `0`.

31. Add the condition `Compare text` for the `txtMessage` object to check if the text is equal to `"Free Ball"` and then invert the condition.

32. Give this event the `Set visible` action to make the `txtMessage` object `Invisible`, as in the following screenshot:

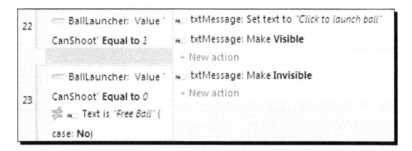

33. Create another event, this time checking if the `BallLauncher` variable `"ComboActivated"` is equal to `1`.

34. Use actions to set the text of `txtMessage` to `"2x Combo"` and make it visible.

35. Add another event and use the condition **Is overlapping another object** for the `Ball` object to check if it is overlapping `BucketCatch`.

36. Insert actions again to set the text of `txtMessage` to `"Free Ball"` and make it visible, as shown in the following screenshot:

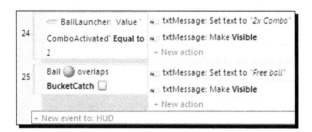

What just happened?

Now our game has events to pick 12 random `Peg` objects to use as green pegs on startup and selects a blue combo peg at the start of each shot. We also put in the events to speed up time with the right button of the mouse while a shot is not being taken.

Let's take a closer look at what's going on.

The For loop

We use a `For` loop to select the random 12 green pegs at the start of the layout. This `For` loop will loop from its start number of 1 to the end number 12 (as `GreenLeft` is equal to 12). We then use a sub-event to pick a random peg that is currently playing the `"Normal"` animation and set it to `"Green"`.

Set timescale

We used the `Set timescale` action to allow the user to speed up time between shots with the right mouse button. The timescale affects how fast the game and sound effects play; a value below 1 will slow down the game, while a value above 1 speeds it up. We use this to let the player adjust the position of the bucket before they shoot.

Portals: a way of getting from A to B

Our player now has a fairly playable game, but with the introduction of portals we can increase the skill required and the chance of getting a high-scoring shot. Portals can be used to make any level easier or more challenging for the player.

Time for action – teleporting the ball

We're going to add an event to teleport the ball to the red portal when it hits the green portal. This will give an added challenge, but also an added reward for the skilled players.

1. Create a new event in the `Game` group for the `Ball` object when it overlaps the `PortalIn` object.

2. Add the **Trigger once while true** condition from the `System` object to this event.

3. Insert an action to set the value of `VelocityX` for the `Ball` object to `Ball[Physics].VelocityX`. This will store its horizontal speed.

4. Add another action to set the value of `VelocityY` for the `Ball` object to `Ball[Physics].VelocityY`. This will store its vertical speed.

5. Create the action `Set immovable` for the `Physics` behavior of the `Ball` object and choose **Yes**.

6. Use the `Set position to another object` action for the `Ball` object to move it to the `PortalOut` object.

7. Create the `Set immovable` action for the `Ball` again to change it back to **No**.

8. Finally, use the `Set velocity` action of the `Physics` behavior for the `Ball` object to set the `X` component to `Ball.Value('VelocityX')` and the value of `Y` component to `Ball.Value('VelocityY')`, as in the following screenshot:

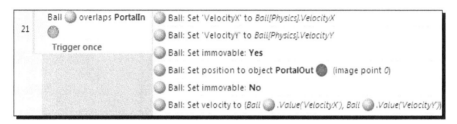

What just happened?

Our ball now teleports to the other portal when it hits the green `PortalIn` object. Although, logically, repositioning and maintaining the velocity of the ball should have all the required actions. The `Physics` behavior in Construct Classic reacts badly without the `Set immovable` actions. In game development, bugs are a natural and inevitable part of the equation, but most of the time there is a work-around or some way to avoid them. As with any program, always remember to save your work frequently and make backups often.

Particle objects: creating a fireworks finale

Our player will want a visual cue when they've won the game. We'll give them this using the particle object to create fireworks. Particle objects can be used in any situation where a large amount of sprites are needed to be emitted, as long as they are not required to collide with other objects. This is because they have been optimized for displaying large amounts of images, rather than acting as game objects.

Time for action – creating fireworks

Right now, our game will stop when the player runs out of balls or completes the level. We'll change this by adding in the win and lose events, as well as a fireworks finale when they win the level.

1. Return to the **Layout Editor,** and on the `Objects` layer, insert a `Particles` object.

2. Name this object `Fireworks` and scroll down to configure the particle settings as shown in the following screenshot. Collapsed groups remain at their default settings.

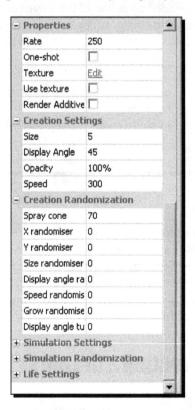

3. Now drag two additional fireworks objects from the `Objects` bar and position the three of them along the bottom, as shown in the following screenshot:

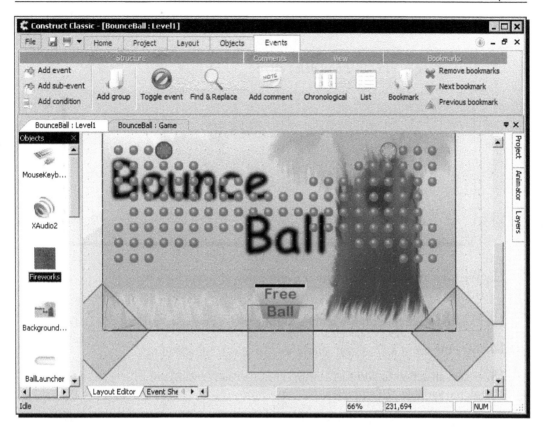

4. Return to the Game event sheet, and in the Start of layout event, add the action Set visible for the Fireworks object and choose **Invisible**.

5. Scrolling down, create a new event at the bottom of the Game group. Select the highlighted **Compare** condition from the System object to compare if Ball.Count is Lower or equal to 0.

6. Add an additional condition to compare the private variable BallsLeft of the BallLauncher object to check if it is Less or equal to 0.

7. Next, create another condition to check if the global variable GreenLeft is Greater than the value 0.

8. Give this event a sub-event with the condition **Trigger once while true** from the System object. This will be used later to play a game over sound.

9. Create another sub-event for the main event to check if the left button of the mouse was clicked.

10. Add an action to this to set the global variable `TotalScore` to 0.

11. Next, add the action `Go to layout` from the `System` object and enter the layout number `LayoutNumber` and delay of `500`.

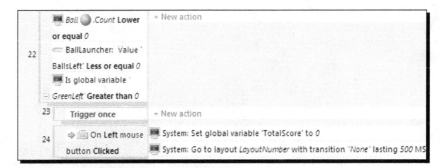

12. We then want to create another event below this one for when `Ball.Count` is `Lower or equal` to 0, but `GreenLeft` is also `Less or equal` to 0.

13. Create an action for this event for setting the `Fireworks` back to `Visible`.

14. Give the event a `Trigger once while true` sub-event.

15. Insert an action to add `BallLauncher.Value('BallsLeft') * 200` to the global variable `TotalScore`.

16. Create two actions for the `BallLauncher` object to set `BallsLeft` to 0 and `CanShoot` to 0.

17. Next, create another sub-event for the main event to check again if the left button of the mouse is clicked.

18. Create a `Next layout` action from the `System` object with a delay of `500` for this sub-event, as shown in the following screenshot:

19. Create a new event for the `HUD` group with the highlighted **Compare** condition for the `System` object. Check if `Ball.Count` is `Lower or equal` to 0.

20. Compare the private variable `BallsLeft` of the `BallLauncher` object to check if it is `Less or equal` to 0.

21. Add another condition to the event to compare the global variable `GreenLeft` to being `Greater than` the value 0.

22. Give this event the highlighted action `Set text` for `txtMessage` and enter the text `"Game Over. Click to restart."`.

23. Create another action to set the `txtMessage` object to `Visible`.

24. Create another event for the HUD group with conditions to check if `Ball.Count` is `Lower or equal` to 0 and `GreenLeft` is also `Less or equal` to 0.

25. Set the text of `txtMessage` to `"Level complete. Click for next level."` and make the object `Visible`, as in the following screenshot:

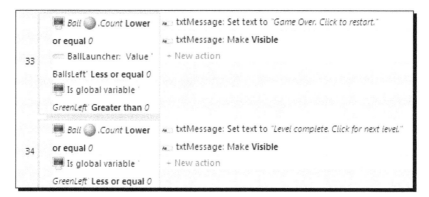

What just happened?

We now have a fireworks display and a message that appears when the player wins the level. We also created events to restart the level if the player gets a game over (at the cost of their total score) or continue to the next level if they've won.

We planned ahead a little and created a `Trigger once while true` event for playing the game over sound, which we'll be adding next.

Playing the sounds and music

Our game is only lacking sound effects and music for the Game event sheet to be complete. Although our player may have music of their own in the background, sound effects provide a unique response to actions and events that the player is currently lacking. This is why we'll be adding them in.

Time for action – adding the sounds and music

We want to give our player some added feedback, so we'll be playing sounds when certain events happen in the game.

1. First, we'll need our sound and music files. Create or find an MP3 song you'd like to loop in the background and name it Game.mp3 before moving it into the same folder as the project source.

2. Next, create sound effects for when the ball is launched, hits a peg, lands in the free ball bucket, hits a combo peg, touches a portal, and when the game is won or lost. Name these Launch.wav, Peg.wav, FreeBall.wav, Combo.wav, Portal.wav, Win.wav, and Lose.wav respectively. Place these in the project source folder as well.

3. Return to the Game event sheet. In the Start of layout event, add the highlighted action **Play music from file** for the XAudio2 object and enter AppPath & "Game.mp3".

4. Add another action to loop the music from the XAudio2 object, as in the following screenshot:

5. Scroll down to event **6** (the event that triggers when the ball hits a peg) and add the highlighted action `Autoplay file` from the `XAudio2` object. Enter the sound file of `AppPath & "Peg.wav"` and click on **Finish**.

6. Go to the sub-event where the animation `"SpecialHit"` is playing and add another `Autoplay file` action to play the file `AppPath & "Combo.wav"`, as in the following screenshot:

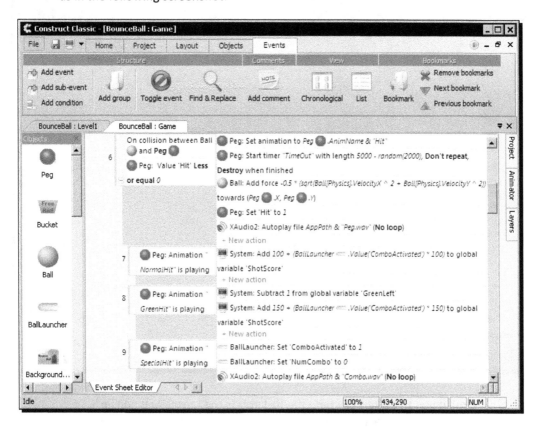

7. Move to event **10**, where the `BallLauncher` private variable `CanShoot` is `Greater than` the value `0`. In the sub-event where the left button of the mouse is clicked to launch the ball. Use the highlighted action `Autoplay file` again to play the file `AppPath & "Launch.wav"`.

8. Scroll down to event **21**, where the ball enters the portal, and add an `Autoplay file` action to play the file `AppPath & "Portal.wav"`, as in the following screenshot:

9. Scroll down to the sub-event **23** where we created an empty `Trigger once while true` event. Create an action to play the sound file `AppPath & "Lose.wav"`, as shown in the following screenshot:

10. Finally, scroll to sub-event `26` and add an `Autoplay file` action to play the sound file `AppPath & "Win.wav"` and drag it to the top, as shown in the following screenshot:

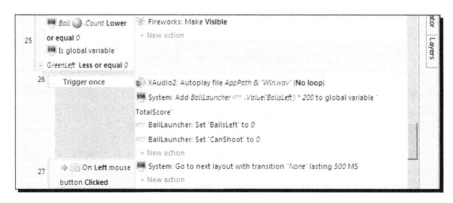

What just happened?

We have now finished the Game event sheet by including the events to play sounds. This makes our game fully functional and leaves only the task of making additional levels.

Creating another level

Like any game, only playing the same level over and over again can become very boring. In our first game, we had to create a whole new game to play a different level. Now we can learn how to create additional levels the correct way and make a better game because of it.

Time for action – making another level

To make the length of our game longer, we'll add a new level for our player to enjoy.

1. Draw up a new 800x600 background image for the new level; an example is shown in the following screenshot:

2. Go into the **Project** menu and right-click on the **Level1** layout and select **Clone layout** from the context menu. Rename the new layout to Level2, and rename the new event sheet to Level2 events.

3. Delete the BackgroundImg object from the new layout in order to replace it with a new one named BackgroundImg2 on the Background layer.

4. Set up the new background object in a similar fashion to the first one, but with the new image.

5. Enable **Snap-to moving** for the grid size of 34x34 again, and position the portal and peg objects as you wish.

6. Finally, in the **Event Sheet Editor**, include the Game event sheet. You can now test your game, as shown in the following screenshot, and play through to the second level:

What just happened?

We were able to take our first layout and create a clone of it to change into our second level. This speeds up the process of making new levels greatly, and through the shared Game event sheet, we don't need to make any more events to do it.

Have a go hero – create additional levels

Now that we know how to make extra levels, why not make a few more and see which of your friends can make it through them all? Remember to use a different name for each background image object and you're ready to go.

Meet the debugger

We have now created a working game, but sometimes there may be a bug we will not understand. This is where the debugger built into Construct Classic comes to help. The debugger allows us to look at memory values and see how many instances of each object we have.

Time for action – looking through the debugger

We may not have had any bugs in this game, but there is usually a point in making games where the debugger might provide some useful information.

1. Open the **Project** tab of the ribbon at the top and click on **Debug all** to start debugging for our game. This will provide the following (or similar) warning messages. These can be ignored as they simply state that a condition refers to an empty value. Click on **OK** to skip these.

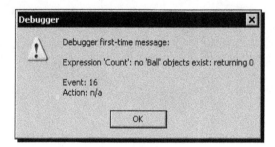

2. Our game is now playing, and we have a **Runtime Debugger** screen to view our different objects and values, as in the following screenshot:

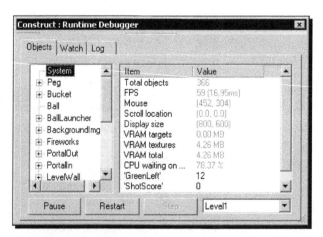

3. By expanding and clicking on items on the left, values can be read off the right side of the screen. Values on the right side of the screen can also be right-clicked to bring up an option to put them on the **Watch** screen, where they can be quickly viewed without clicking through the left menu to find them again.

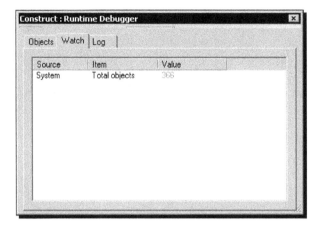

4. Finally, the **Log** screen will show all previous pop ups given by the debugger, as in the following screenshot:

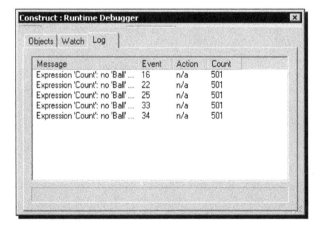

What just happened?

We've now had a look around the debugger. This tool starts up whenever you select the options **Debug all** or **Debug layout**, with the second option starting the debugger for a single layout. The debugger can also be used to Pause and Step through the game in order to view the minor changes.

Pop quiz – physical games

Let's try a multiple choice pop quiz to see how much we remember of the chapter.

1. What do we do to use the Physics engine in a game?

    a. Add the Physics object to the layout

    b. Add a Physics behavior for each object

    c. Check the Physics option for each object

2. What settings do we use to stop the Physics engine from rotating an object?

    a. Check No Rotation

    b. Check Immovable

    c. Set the objects **Angle** settings to No rotation

3. How do we stop an object from being pushed by other Physics engine objects?

    a. Set **Contact friction** to 100%

    b. Use events to ignore the collision

    c. Set the **Mass** of the largest object to be much larger than the objects that will collide with it

Summary

We learned a lot in this chapter while making our BounceBall game. In general, we learned how to use the Physics behavior, use event sheets, and play across multiple levels. We started by learning how to give our objects the Physics behavior and using events to control it. In doing so, we also came across event sheets and groups, which make our events more manageable.

We then saw how to teleport objects with the Physics behavior, and we also learned to use the Particles object to create our fireworks finale. We finished the chapter by gaining the skills necessary for creating additional levels and transitioning to them, as well as using the debugger to see if there are any bugs in our game. We also discussed some useful expressions such as Clamp and Set timescale.

We are now ready to learn about loading and making custom levels, which is the next chapter.

6
Custom Levels

We have a game with multiple levels, but we would need to export a brand new EXE each time we add a new one. Instead of that, we'll load additional levels from a file and make a level editor to save to it. These skills will be useful for any future games we make and can extend the life of our BounceBall game.

In this chapter, we shall:

- ◆ Learn what an INI file is and how they work
- ◆ Modify our BounceBall game to load level data from an INI file
- ◆ Add a game over screen for when all levels are complete
- ◆ Create a BounceBall Level Editor and save our level data to an INI file

So let's get on with it.

The user friendly INI file

An INI file is an extremely easy way to save information. It stores all data in a file as plain text, so it can be edited from any text editor. We'll need to know how these are stored and used before we can continue making our game.

Time for action – creating an INI file

We'll create an INI file using Notepad to understand how they work. In doing so, we'll also make a test level we can load later in `BounceBall`.

1. Open up `Notepad` (normally found in **Start | All Programs | Accessories**) and then use **File | Save As...**.

2. Navigate to the folder where `BounceBall` is saved, and enter the **File name** of `Levels.INI` and set the **Save as type** to **All Files**. Click on **Save**:

3. Now we can begin entering the level details. Type the text `[Game]` on the first line as the group and then press *Enter*.

4. Next, type `NumCustomLevels=1` and move down a line again.

5. We can then add data for the first level. Write the text `[CustomLevel1]` and press *Enter*.

6. We are now defining the values of the level. Fill the first line of the level with the text `Background=Back3.png` and move to the next line.

7. Use this next line to set the number of pegs to be created for the level. Enter the line `NumPegs=12`.

8. Now we can fill in the X and Y positions of objects in this level. In order to do this, fill in the remaining text as shown in the following screenshot:

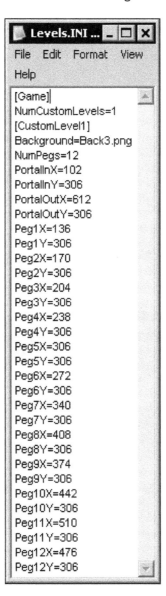

What just happened?

We have created our first INI file and level. We did this to create test data for when we add level loading to our BounceBall game. This also gave us the ability to see the data structure of our levels and see what an INI file looks like.

Now we can look at the key features of an INI file.

INI groups

INI files use square brackets to separate groups of data. Our first group was [Game], which we used to define how many levels are stored in the INI file.

INI items

All data is stored as items in groups. We use item names to hold the data. For instance, the NumPegs item will hold the number of pegs to create for that level. Then we assign each peg an X and Y position. These item names cannot be repeated within their group, but can be used again in another group (or in our case, another level).

Loading levels

We may have written the INI file we'll use for a level, but our game doesn't load it yet. So, this means we'll need to add to our BounceBall game in order to load the new levels. This is useful as the user can then play a vast number of levels, through the INI file.

Time for action – load custom levels

We are now going to modify our game to load levels from the INI file. This will allow us to add and remove levels at will, as well as share them with friends.

1. Open the BounceBall project again and clone the last level layout using the technique we learned in *Chapter 5, Practical Physics*.

2. Name this layout LevelINI and its event sheet to LevelINI Events.

3. Delete the background image object and create a new one. This time, name it `BackgroundINI` and use a default image for it (to show the correct image has not loaded, or no image exists). A **No Image** example is shown in the following screenshot, named `BackNA.png`:

4. Now, also create the background image that we will use for our first custom level and name it `Back3.png` (as we entered in the INI file). Save this to the `BounceBall` project folder and return to Construct Classic:

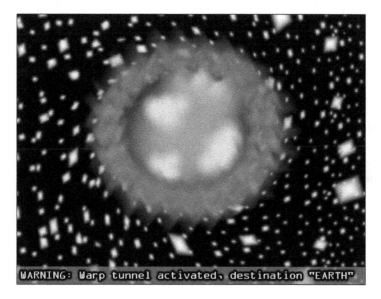

5. Next, delete all but one of the `Peg` objects on the new layout, and move this last peg outside of the layout.

6. Then move both the `PortalIn` and `PortalOut` objects outside the layout.

7. Insert the `INI` object into the layout on the `Objects` layer.

8. Add another global variable to the project, this time use the name `CurrentINILevel` and default value 1.

9. Now switch over to the **Event Sheet Editor** for this layout and create a `Start of layout` event.

10. Add the action `Set INI file` for the `INI` object and enter `AppPath &` `"Levels.ini"` in the parameter box.

11. Add another action to this event. Choose the `Peg` object and select **Destroy**.

12. Next, create a sub-event for the `System` object condition `Compare global variable`. **Compare that** `CurrentINILevel` **is** `Less or equal to` `INI.` `ItemValue("Game", "NumCustomLevels")` **and click on Finish**.

13. **Create the action** `Load animation frame from file` **for the** `BackgroundINI` **object and enter the parameter of** `AppPath & INI.ItemString("CustomLevel"` `& global('CurrentINILevel'), "Background")`.

14. **Add another action to this sub-event. This time select the** `PortalIn` **object and give it the action** `Set position`. **Enter the** X **value of** `INI.` `ItemValue("CustomLevel" & global('CurrentINILevel'),` `"PortalInX")` **and** Y **value of** `INI.ItemValue("CustomLevel" &` `global('CurrentINILevel'), "PortalInY")` **before clicking on Finish**.

15. **Add a similar action for the** `PortalOut` **object, this time setting the** X **value to** `INI.ItemValue("CustomLevel" & global('CurrentINILevel'),` `"PortalOutX")` **and the** Y **value to** `INI.ItemValue("CustomLevel" &` `global('CurrentINILevel'), "PortalOutY")`.

16. In order to create and position the `Peg` objects, create another sub-event below the current one. Use the `System` condition `For` and enter a loop name of `"LoadPegs"`. Have this loop go from 1 to `INI.ItemValue("CustomLevel" &` `global('CurrentINILevel'), "NumPegs")`.

17. Now create an action for this sub-event from the `System` object. Choose the highlighted action `Create object` to spawn a `Peg` object on the `"Objects"` layer with `X` position `INI.ItemValue("CustomLevel" & global('CurrentINILevel'), "Peg" & LoopIndex & "X")` and `Y` position `INI.ItemValue("CustomLevel" & global('CurrentINILevel'), "Peg" & LoopIndex & "Y")`.

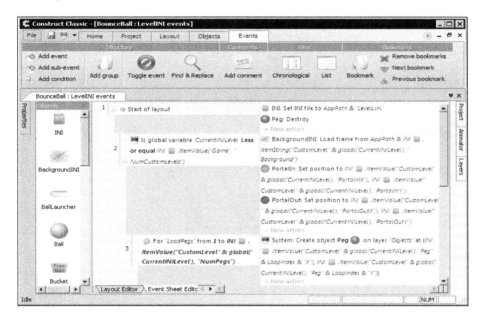

18. Next, create another sub-event for the `Start of layout` event. Choose the `System` condition `Else` and click on **Finish**.

19. For this event, add the `System` action `Go to layout` and enter the layout number `0` before clicking on **Finish**.

20. In order to complete the event sheet, right-click and include the event sheet `Game`:

21. Now, add a new layout to the project. Name this layout `NextINI` and its event sheet as `NextINI events`.

22. Switch to the **Event Sheet Editor** for this layout and add a `Start of layout` event.

23. Insert the `System` action `Add to value` to add 1 to `CurrentINILevel`.

24. Finally, add the `System` action `Previous layout` to the event:

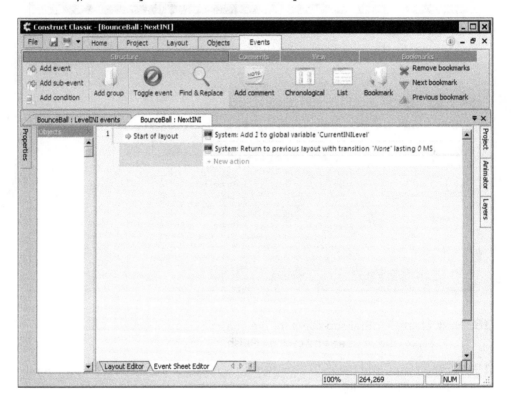

What just happened?

We can now load up as many custom levels as our INI file can hold. We used the `LevelINI` layout to load and play the level and the `NextINI` layout to handle level changing without needing to touch any events in our `Game` event sheet.

It is important to note that as we have now added level loading, all future levels must be added to the INI file (rather than the project source). This is due to the `LevelINI` layout ending the game when all INI levels are finished.

Now, we can look closer at what we did to load the levels.

Setting the INI file

At the start of the layout, we set the INI file to our `Levels.INI` file. We do this so that all future data is pulled from this file. This action can be used any time in a game to change between multiple INI files, rather than needing many different INI objects.

Loading the level

If the `CurrentINILevel` value is lower or equal to the number of levels (as stated in the `Game` group of the INI file), we start placing objects in the level. Otherwise we exit the game.

The `CurrentINILevel` value is also used to decide which level group to pull the level data from. This means the line `"CustomLevel" & global('CurrentINILevel')` translates to the group `CustomLevel1` for our first level.

The first action lets us load our background image into the `BackgroundINI` object. We then go on to set the positions of the `PortalIn` and `PortalOut` objects before starting the `For` loop sub-event.

This for loop `LoadPegs` goes through the number of pegs in the level file and creates them at their specified X and Y position.

We use `LoopIndex` to get the current index of the `For` loop in order to select each peg up to `NumPegs`. During the first run of the loop, the X position `"Peg" & LoopIndex & "X"` would get the value of Peg1X from our INI file.

Including the Game event sheet

After we've done all this, we include the `Game` event sheet to start the game with our loaded level. Event sheets are processed from top to bottom, and hence all of our loading events are performed before the `Game` event sheet begins. The game event sheet will still perform its `Start of layout` event as well.

The NextINI layout

This layout is a simple redirect to increase the INI level and send the player back to the `LevelINI` layout to play it. This is used so that no changes have to be made to the base `Game` event sheet.

The Game Over screen

Our game is nearly complete, but we should add an ending screen so the player can see their final score before the game quits. As an added plus, we can insert a textbox to inform the player of the level editor (which we'll be making next) that they can use to add more levels to the game.

Time for action – creating the Game Over layout

We'll use a Game Over layout to show the player their final score and tell them that they have completed all of the (currently) existing levels.

1. On this layout, we will have a randomly positioned firework with accompanying firework sound. Create a sound that you would like to be played when the firework explodes and name it `Firework.wav` before placing it in the project folder.

2. Create a new layout for our project and name it `GameOver`. Also, rename the event sheet to `GameOver events`.

3. Select a `Layout color` for the layout by selecting it and viewing its properties. The color `LightBlue` works well.

4. Create three text objects, `txtCongratulations`, `txtUseEditor`, and `txtFinalScore`, for this layout. Have their `Horizontal alignment` values set to `Center` and set the texts, colors, and positions of these objects to those shown in the following screenshot:

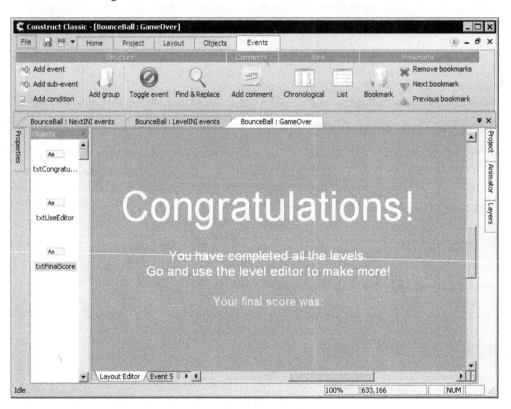

5. Next, create another text object and put it in the bottom-left corner. Name this as `txtExitKeys` and set its text to `Press any key to exit`.

6. Next, create a `Particles` object and name it `VictoryFirework`.

7. In the **Attributes** of this object, check **Destroy on startup**.

8. Next, set the **Rate** property to `400` and check both `One-Shot` and **Render Additive**:

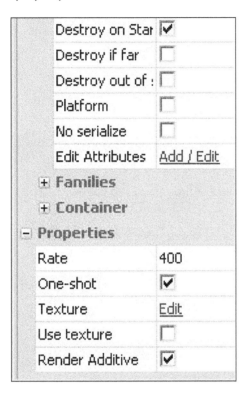

9. Further down the properties of our object, set the **Size**, **Display Angle**, **Opacity**, and **Speed** to 5, 45, 80%, and 300 respectively.

10. Next, set the **Spray Cone** to 360 and the **Speed randomizer** to -250:

Creation Settings	
Size	5
Display Angle	45
Opacity	80%
Speed	300
Creation Randomization	
Spray cone	360
X randomiser	0
Y randomiser	0
Size randomiser	0
Display angle rand	0
Speed randomiser	-250

11. Set the **Destroy mode** of the particles to Particle stopped and the **Fade out time** to 800.

12. Next, pick a **Color** and **Fade to color** for the firework; WebWhite and WebGreen are the example colors:

Destroy mode	Particle stopped
Color	WebWhite
Fade to color	WebGreen
Fade colour time	1000
Fade out time	800
Timeout	1000

13. We are now ready to create the events for this layout. Switch to the **Event Sheet Editor** and create a Start of layout event.

14. Create an action for this event. Under the **XAudio2** object list of actions, select **Pause Music**.

15. Following that create an action to set the text of `txtFinalScore` to `"Your final score was: " & global('TotalScore')`.

16. Next, create an event for the `MouseKeyboard` object and select the condition `On any key pressed`.

17. Give this event the `System` action `Close`.

18. Create another event, this time selecting the `System` condition `Every X Milliseconds`. Enter the time value of `2000` milliseconds (2 seconds).

19. Create the highlighted `System` action `Create object` to create our `VictoryFirework` object at the X position `random(DisplayWidth)` and Y position `random(DisplayHeight)`.

20. Next, insert the highlighted action `Autoplay file` for the `XAudio2` object to play the file `AppPath & "Firework.wav"`:

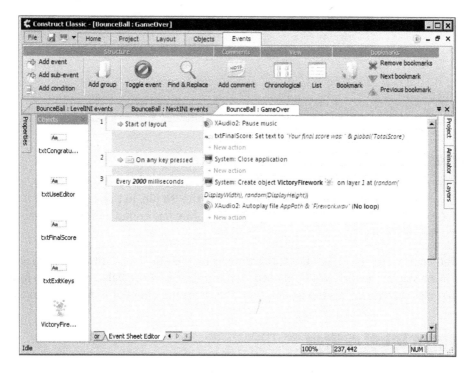

21. Before finishing, go back to the `LevelINI` event sheet and change the `Go to layout` action destination layout number to the last layout of your project. For example, if no additional levels were created beyond those of this book, then this number would be `5`.

22. Finally, we can now export our completed BounceBall game:

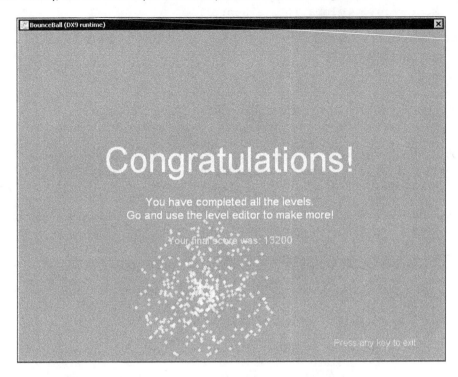

What just happened?

We have now finished all of the events and layouts for our BounceBall game. Any future levels we want to add will be created by using the INI file. In this section, we added a Game Over screen to inform the player the game has ended and reward them with a final high score.

We added another Particles object, this time using the One-shot attribute to make it behave like a single firework. We then used a Speed randomizer value of -250 to have some particles slow down or stop on creation. This gives the effect of a solid circle explosion.

Making a level editor

We now have our BounceBall game completed, but we will want to create a level editor for it to make adding new levels easier. This will let both us and our players create levels with ease.

Our game may load levels, but even making a 12 peg level in Notepad can get tiresome. We're going to change this by creating a graphical level editor from scratch. This section will be a bit longer than normal, so we'll be using subsections to help group the steps together.

Time for action – creating the objects

We will now create the objects for our level editor. This will be similar to the objects we've made in our `BounceBall` game, but will also include the Graphical User Interface (GUI) objects for easy map editing.

1. Before making the editor, calculate the corners of where pegs and portals can be placed in your level editor. This can be done by taking a peg in the `BounceBall` project and moving it to the top-left and bottom-right corners of the target play area and recording its X and Y position. In this book, the smallest peg X and Y values allowed will be `34,170`, and the largest will be `714,476`.

2. Start a new Construct Classic project and set its application name to `BounceBall Level Editor`. Save this as `Editor.cap` in your project folder.

3. Rename the starting layout to `Editor` and its event sheet to `Editor events`.

4. On this layout, create 4 layers: `EditorHUD`, `EditorObjects`, `Objects`, and `Background`, with `EditorHUD` being topmost.

5. Next, create three global variables, the first being `CurrentLevel` with a value of `1`, then `CurrentObject` with a value of `1`, and finally `CurrentBackground` with a text of `NA`.

6. On the `EditorObjects` layer, create the `Mouse & Keyboard` object, as well as an INI object and `Function` object. Rename the INI object as `LevelINI`.

7. Now, we can create the graphical objects of the layout. Start on the `Background` layer and recreate the `BackgroundINI` object from our `BounceBall` cap file. Note that copying this object from the `BounceBall.cap` file will not work as Construct Classic does not allow copying between different source files.

8. Next, move to the `Objects` layer and create the sprites `Peg`, `PortalIn`, and `PortalOut`. Have them take the same size as their counterparts in `BounceBall`, but do not add any behaviors to them.

9. Give these objects the `Solid` and `Destroy on Startup` attributes.

10. Moving up to the `EditorObjects` layer, create a sprite named `Cursor` and give it 3 animation frames. The first frame should have the `Peg` object image, the second `PortalIn`, and the third `PortalOut`.

11. Set the **Animation speed** to 0 and return to the `Cursor` object properties to set its **Opacity** to 80% and **Filter** to `LightGrey`. Check the **Solid** attribute for this object as well.

12. Next, create a `Box` object and name it `EditRegion`. Set its **Hotspot** property to the `Top-Left` and its `X` and `Y` position to the minimum that we had recorded earlier (in the case of the book: `34, 170`).

13. Uncheck the box for **Transparent fill**. Then set **Colour 1** and **Colour 2** to `WebMediumSeaGreen` and the **Fill** color to `WebLimeGreen`.

14. Next, using our maximum X and Y position recordings, calculate the width and height of the edit region object. Subtract the minimum X and Y values from their respective maximums to get the width and height to set the edit region. Using this book's values, the box size is calculated as a `Width` of `714` and `Height` of `306`.

15. For easier object placement, add `10` to each of the `Width` and `Height` values for the `EditRegion` object.

16. Next, set the opacity of the **EditRegion** object to `40%`. The layout should look similar to the following screenshot:

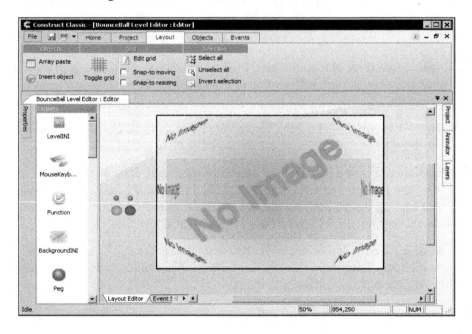

17. Now move on to the `EditorHUD` layer. Create a `Panel` object and name it `panHUD`.

18. Set the `Filter bottom-left` and `Filter bottom-right` settings of the `Panel` object to `Blue-Grey`.

19. Place the panel object in the bottom-left with a height of `100` and stretch it horizontally across to the other edge of the layout.

20. Create a text object named `txtLevel`, and set its text to `Level: 1` and place it in the top-left of the `panHUD` object.

21. Create two `Button` objects below the `txtLevel` object. The first being `btnNext` with `Button text` of `Next`, and `btnPrevious` with text `Previous`.

22. Next to these buttons, create another two with the names `btnSave` and `btnLoad`. Set the text of `btnSave` to `Save Level` and `btnLoad` to `Load/Clear`.

23. Following that, create another two text objects next to the new buttons. This time, name them `txtSaveResult` and `txtBackImage`.

24. Enter a text as `Error: 12 pegs required` for `txtSaveResult` and `Background Image:` for `txtBackImage`. Check the property **Invisible on start** for this object.

25. Now, create an `Edit Box` and name it `ediBackground`. Place this object next to the `txtBackImage` box.

26. Then set the objects `Properties` to those as shown in the following screenshot:

Properties	
Auto scroll horizon	☑
Auto scroll vertical	☐
Border	☑
Enabled	☑
Horizontal scrollbaɪ	☐
Initial text	Back3.png
Lowercase	☐
Multiline	☐
Password mode	☐
Uppercase	☐
Vertical scrollbar	☐

27. Next, create another `Button` object of the name `btnLoadBack` and set its text to `Load Image`. Position this button next to the edit box object.

28. Now create another three buttons of the names `btnPeg`, `btnPortalIn`, and `btnPortalOut`. Have the text of these buttons be `Peg`, `Portal In`, and `Portal Out` respectively.

29. Now create the text object `txtEditRegion` and set its text to `Objects can only be placed within the green region`. Position this object above the three buttons.

30. Then create the text object `txtControls` with two lines of text. On the first line, have `Left click - Place object`, and on the second line `Right click - Remove object`. Have this object at the top-right of the `panHUD` object.

31. We now have our objects for the level editor ready. The layout of these objects should look similar to the following screenshot:

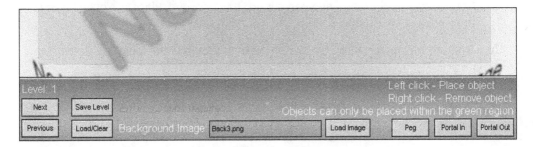

Time for action – loading and saving levels with events

Now we are going to add the events into our editor to load and save levels to INI files.

1. Now we can switch over to the **Event Sheet Editor** to start the events for our editor. Start by creating a `Start of layout` event to set the INI file to `AppPath & "Levels.ini"`.

2. Following that, create a sub-event for this to check if the global variable `CurrentLevel` is `Less or equal` to `LevelINI.ItemValue("Game", "NumCustomLevels")`.

3. Create the action `Call function` of the `Function` object to call `"LoadLevel"`, a function we'll be using to load the level objects and background.

4. Next, create a new event with the `MouseKeyboard` condition `Mouse is over object?` to check if the mouse is overlapping the `EditRegion` object.

5. For this event, create the action `Set visible` for the `EditRegion` object to make it `Invisible`.

6. Next, add the `System` action `Set group enabled` to set the group `"Level Objects"` to enabled. We'll use this group later to handle the placing and removal of objects.

7. Next, create actions to set the `Cursor` object to `Visible` and the `txtEditRegion` object to `Invisible`.

8. Then add the `MouseKeyboard` action `Set cursor visible` to make the mouse cursor `Invisible`.

9. Now create another event with the `System` condition `Else`.

10. Give this event the same actions as above, but with an inverse result. This means the `EditRegion` object and mouse cursor become visible, while the other objects are made invisible. The group `"Level Objects"` is also disabled. Our events should so far match the following screenshot:

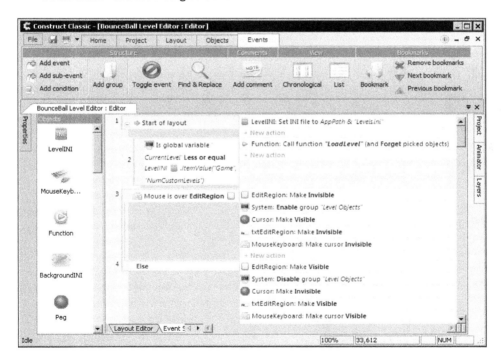

11. Next, create three events to check that the level objects are overlapping the EditRegion (Peg, PortalIn, and PortalOut). Invert their conditions, and in each case destroy the object that isn't overlapping the level region. A screenshot of these events is shown as follows:

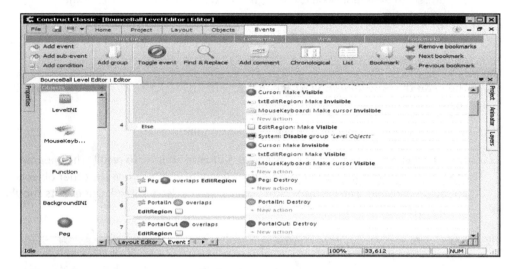

12. Now create a group named as Save and load with the description Events for saving and loading maps.

13. In this group, create an event for the Function object with the condition On function and parameter "LoadLevel".

14. Create an action for this event to load the BackgroundINI frame from AppPath & LevelINI.ItemString("CustomLevel" & global('CurrentLevel'), "Background").

15. Next, add another action to set the global variable CurrentBackground to LevelINI.ItemString("CustomLevel" & global('CurrentLevel'), "Background").

16. We can now add an action to create the PortalIn object on the "Objects" layer with an X of LevelINI.ItemValue("CustomLevel" & global('CurrentLevel'), "PortalInX") and Y position LevelINI.ItemValue("CustomLevel" & global('CurrentLevel'), "PortalInY").

17. Then create another action for the PortalOut object with an X position of LevelINI.ItemValue("CustomLevel" & global('CurrentLevel'), "PortalOutX") and Y of LevelINI.ItemValue("CustomLevel" & global('CurrentLevel'), "PortalOutY").

18. Adding the final action of the event, set the text of the `ediBackground` object to `global('CurrentBackground')`.

19. Now add a `for` loop as a sub-event with the name `"LoadPegs"` and loops from 1 to `LevelINI.ItemValue("CustomLevel" & global('CurrentLevel'), "NumPegs")`.

20. Use an action to create a Peg on the objects layer at X position `LevelINI.ItemValue("CustomLevel" & global('CurrentLevel'), "Peg" & LoopIndex & "X")` and Y position of `LevelINI.ItemValue("CustomLevel" & global('CurrentLevel'), "Peg" & LoopIndex & "Y")` for each peg in the level. The new events should look similar to the following screenshot:

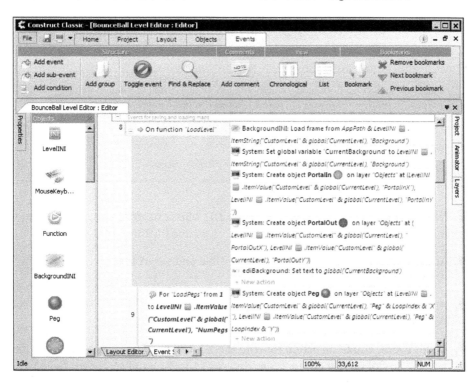

21. Next, add an event for when the function `"SaveLevel"` is called.

22. Add the action `Write string` for the `INI` object and enter the details as shown in the following screenshot:

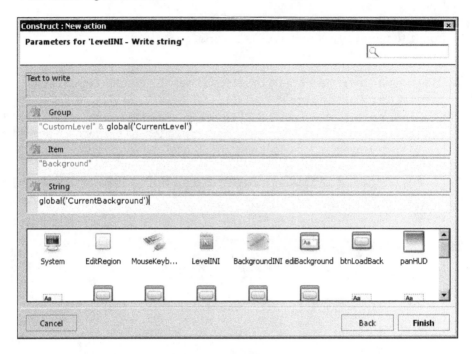

23. Next, add a `Write value` action for the `INI` object to store `Peg.Count` in the item `NumPegs` for the group `"CustomLevel" & global('CurrentLevel')`.

24. Add actions to make `txtSaveResult` visible and set its text to `"Save successful"`.

25. Now add a sub-event with the highlighted `System` condition `Compare` to check if `PortalIn.Count + PortalOut.Count` is equal to `2`.

26. In this event, create an action to write the `X` position of `PortalIn.X` to the item `PortalInX` of the INI group `"CustomLevel" & global('CurrentLevel')`. Do the same for the `Y` position of the `PortalIn` object (saving `PortalIn.Y` to `PortalInY`) as well.

27. Now add actions to store the position of the `PortalOut` object (`PortalOutX` and `PortalOutY` accordingly). The following screenshot shows how the events should look:

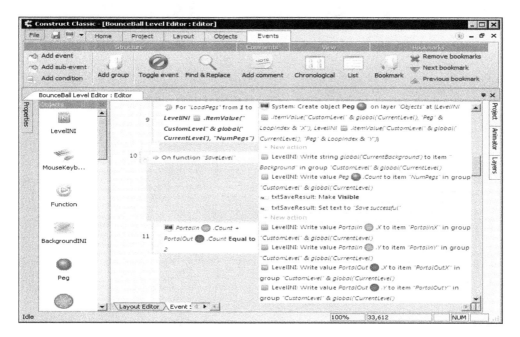

28. Next, create an `else` event for when there is an incomplete pair of portals.

29. Create actions for this event to save the `PortalIn` and `PortalOut` positions as `-1000`. This event is shown as follows:

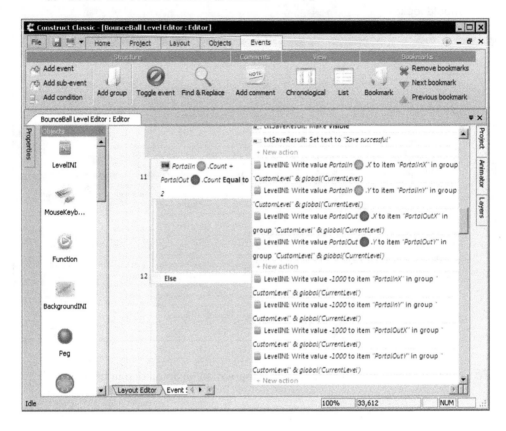

30. Now create another sub-event under the function to check if the global variable `CurrentLevel` is `Greater than` the value of `LevelINI.ItemValue("Game", "NumCustomLevels")`.

31. Create an action to write the value `global('CurrentLevel')` to the item `"NumCustomLevels"` in INI group `Game`.

32. Next, create a sub-event under the save function with the `System` condition `For each object`. Select the `Peg` object and click on **Finish**.

33. Create actions for this sub-event to save the `Peg.X` and `Peg.Y` to items `"Peg"` & `LoopIndex` & `"X"` and `"Peg"` & `LoopIndex` & `"Y"` respectively in the group `"CustomLevel"` & `global('CurrentLevel')`. The following screenshot shows how the events should look:

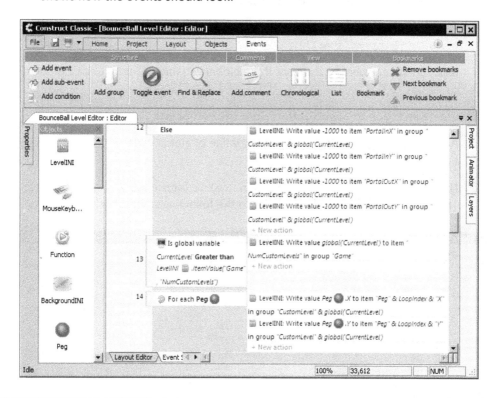

Time for action – creating events for the interface

Now we want to add events to allow the interface controls to perform their intended actions.

1. First, make a group with the name HUD and description `Events for HUD controls`.

2. Create an event in this group to compare that global variable `CurrentLevel` is `Greater than` the value of `LevelINI.ItemValue("Game", "NumCustomLevels")`.

3. Add the action `Disable` for the `btnNext` object.

4. Next, create an action to set the global variable `CurrentLevel` to `LevelINI.ItemValue("Game", "NumCustomLevels") + 1`.

5. Finish the event by adding an action to set the text of `txtLevel` to `"Level: New"`.

6. Now create the `System` event `Else`.

7. Use the action `Enable` for the `btnNext` object.

8. Following that, create an action to set the text of `txtLevel` to `"Level: "` & `global('CurrentLevel')`.

9. Next, create an event to compare if the global variable `CurrentLevel` is `Less or equal` to `1`.

10. Create an action to `Disable` the `btnPrevious` object.

11. Add another action, this time to set the value of global variable `CurrentLevel` to `1`.

12. Now add an `Else` event with the action `Enable` for the `btnPrevious` object. These events should now look similar to the following screenshot:

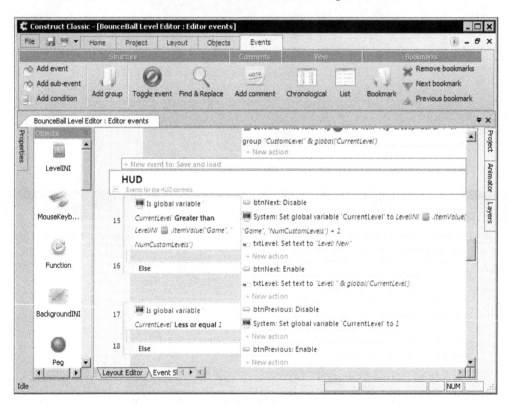

13. Now create an event with the condition On button clicked for the btnSave object.

14. Add a sub-event with the System condition Compare to check if Peg.Count is Greater or equal to 12.

15. Create an action to call the function "SaveLevel".

16. Next, create an Else event for this sub-event.

17. Add an action to make txtSaveResult visible and another to set its text to "Error: 12 pegs required".

18. Now create a new event for when btnLoad is clicked. Give it three actions to destroy the Peg, PortalIn, and PortalOut objects before a final action to call the "LoadLevel" function.

19. Following that, create an event for when btnLoadBack is clicked.

20. Have an action to load the animation frame AppPath & ediBackground.Text into the BackgroundINI object.

21. Next, create an action to set the global variable CurrentBackground to ediBackground.Text. These events should now match the following screenshot:

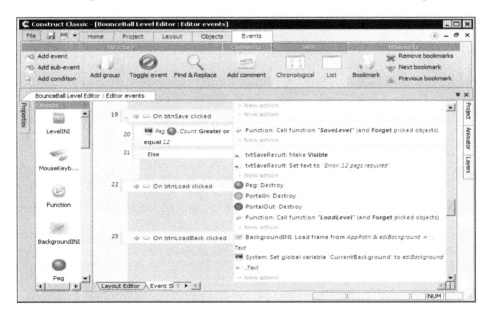

22. Next, create an event to add 1 to the global variable CurrentLevel when btnNext is clicked.

23. Then create another event to subtract 1 from `CurrentLevel` when `btnPrevious` is clicked.

24. Now create three events to set the value of global variable `CurrentObject` to 1, 2, or 3 if `btnPeg`, `btnPortalIn`, or `btnPortalOut` are clicked respectively. The events should now look similar to those as shown in the following screenshot:

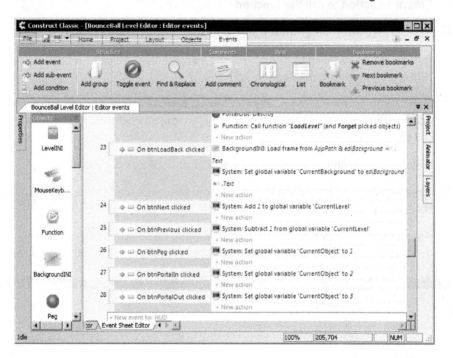

25. Next, create a new group named `Level Objects` with the description `Events for placing and removing objects`. This time, also check the box for **Disable group by default**.

26. Create an `Always` event for this new group.

27. Now add the `Set position` action to the `Cursor` object to set its X position to `int(MouseX / 34) * 34` and Y position to `int(MouseY / 34) * 34`.

28. Then create another action to always set the animation frame of the `Cursor` object to `global('CurrentObject')`.

29. Following that, create a new event to compare if the global variable `CurrentObject` is `Equal` to the value 1.

30. For this event, add two actions: one to set the `Width` of the `Cursor` object to 20 and the other to set its `Height` to 20.

31. Create an `Else` event that instead sets the `Cursor` object width and height to `40`. The events should look similar to the following screenshot:

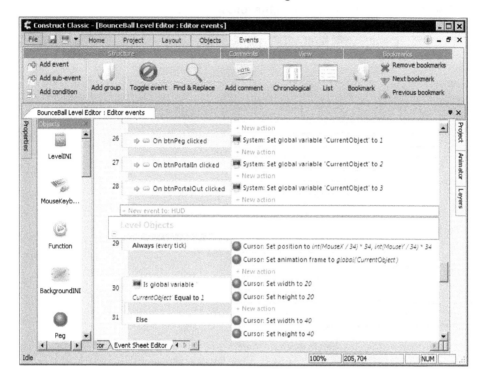

32. Moving on, create another event. This time, select the `MouseKeyboard` condition `On click`. Select the **Left mouse button** and click on **Finish**.

33. Insert a second condition to check if the `Cursor` object is overlapping the object `"Solid"`. `Invert` this condition.

34. Now add a sub-event to compare if the global variable `CurrentObject` is equal to `1`.

35. Give this sub-event the highlighted `System` action `Create object` to create a `Peg` on layer `"Objects"` at `Cursor.X` and `Cursor.Y`.

36. Next, create another sub-event for the main event, this time comparing if `CurrentObject` is equal to `2`.

37. Create an action to destroy the `PortalIn` object and another subsequent action to re-create it at `Cursor.X` and `Cursor.Y` on the `"Objects"` layer.

38. Doing the same for when CurrentObject is equal to 3, have the PortalOut object destroyed and recreated on layer "Objects" at Cursor.X and Cursor.Y. These events should now match the following screenshot:

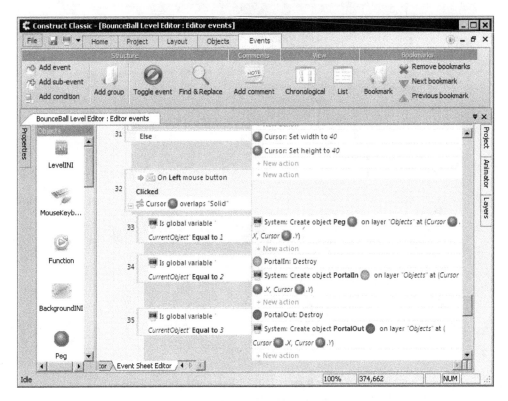

39. Now create an event for when the *Right* mouse button is clicked. Have this event also have a condition for when the Cursor object is overlapping a "Solid" object, but do not invert it.

40. Add a sub-event to check if the Cursor object is overlapping a Peg object, and give it an action to destroy the Peg object.

41. Next, create similar sub-events to check when the Cursor is overlapping the PortalIn and PortalOut objects. Add actions to destroy these objects respectively so that the final events look similar to the following screenshot:

42. Following that, export the project as BounceBall Editor.exe.

43. Finally, use the exported level editor to remake our first custom level and click on **Save**:

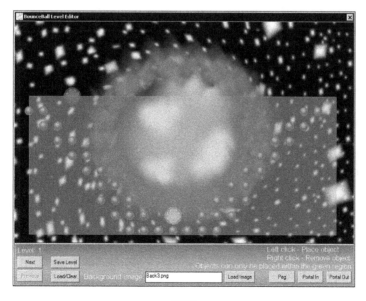

What just happened?

We now have a fully-working level editor for our game, which we can use to make new levels or edit old ones from the INI file. This completed our game and gives our players a way to extend it whenever they want. They can even share the levels they've made by copying them from the `Levels.INI` file.

Now we can take a closer look at some of the things that we did in order to make it.

The edit region

We had to take measurements of the rectangle where we wanted to be able to place objects. However, when we created the edit region object, we went 10 pixels over the target X and Y for the bottom and right sides. This was done as the `Cursor` object was locked to the smallest possible X and Y grid position, and hence moving the mouse a little lower than the target grid point is needed.

We also used this edit region to hide the mouse cursor and show our `Cursor` object instead when the mouse is over the edit region.

The function object

We used the `Function` object to further reuse events and actions in our level editor. Functions are very useful as information can be passed to them in parameters. They can even interact with objects picked in the condition that called the function when `Remember picked objects` is set to `Remember`.

Enabling and disabling groups

We used the group `LevelObjects` to handle the placement and removal of objects. However, we only wanted this to happen when the mouse was over the `EditRegion` object. This is where the ability to enable and disable a group came in handy as we could simply switch those events on and off.

Writing to an INI file

We used two actions to write to the INI file. `Write value` was used when we wanted to store a number, and `Write string` was used to store text data. Whenever INI data doesn't seem to be stored or read right, this might be the area where the problem is!

Positioning the Cursor object to a grid

In order to keep our `Cursor` object in line with the grid, we used the expression `int()` to round the value of the position divided by the grid size (`MouseX / 34`) to a whole number. We then multiply this whole number by the grid size again to get our target position (`int(MouseX / 34) * 34`).

As our grid is square, we used the same method for calculating both X and Y positions, just replacing the X or Y.

Placing portals

When placing the portal objects, we destroy any instances that may already exist of them as each level is to only have one PortalIn and one PortalOut object. When a full pair is not detected on save (`PortalIn.Count` and `PortalOut.Count` would both be equal to 1 and a full pair gives 2), the portals are stored as having X and Y positions `-1000`. This is to keep them far away from the layout and allow for levels without portals.

Have a go hero – make a level editor for your platform game

Now that we've learned how to make additional levels and level editors, use these skills to expand your previous game—the platformer.

Remember to copy the events to a new event sheet and share it between the levels to avoid reinventing the wheel. Some other changes will also be needed to allow INI level loading and level transition when a level is completed.

Pop quiz – INI file recap

Let us try a multiple choice pop quiz to see how much we remember of the chapter.

1. What can be stored in an INI file?

    a. Text only

    b. Text and numbers

    c. Numbers only

    d. Game resources such as music and images

2. How many INI files can be used at once?

    a. Each INI object in a layout can open its own INI file

    b. One INI file can be used at a time

    c. One INI file can be used per game

3. INI files are best used for?

   a. Storing high scores and player statistics securely

   b. Storing images

   c. Storing data for easy modification

Summary

We have finished our `BounceBall` game through learning to make our own custom levels and level editor. These skills can be applied to any future game you make where custom levels would be desired.

In this chapter, we first learned how to create an `INI` file from `Notepad` to learn its base structure, and then how to use that file in Construct Classic to create custom levels. Next, we finished the main game by adding a `Game Over` screen to tell the player their final score and that they have completed the levels. Finally, we went on to learn how to create a level editor, which can save and load `INI` file levels for our `BounceBall` game.

Now that we've finished our second game, we're ready to move on and learn about creating 2D shooters, which just so happens to be the topic of the next chapter.

7
Platformer Revisited, a 2D Shooter

We're now ready to start our final game, a side-scrolling shooter game in the vein of classics such as Contra or Metal Slug. In making this game, we'll learn how to handle multiple players, how to use Construct Classic's shadow engine, and how to create enemies that shoot at the players. This will build upon all the skills we learned in our very first game of this book.

In this chapter, we shall:

- ◆ Learn how to make a two-player platformer
- ◆ Learn how to make objects shoot projectiles and create muzzle flashes
- ◆ Learn how to use parallax to give the impression of depth
- ◆ Learn how to use the built-in lights and shadow casters of Construct Classic
- ◆ Learn to create enemies that shoot projectiles and move towards our players

So let's get on with it.

Before we start

As there is a large amount of ground to cover in this chapter, we'll be moving quickly through steps similar to those we've done before. If it's been a while since you've used Construct, then you may find it useful to read through a chapter or two again before continuing, because certain steps assume that you are able to complete actions we have performed in the past.

Two specific chapters worth looking back on are *Chapter 3, Adding the Challenge* and *Chapter 4, Making Noise* for a recap on what we did when making our first platform game.

Multiplayer: getting your friends involved

In this part of the chapter, we'll create a platformer similar to the first one we made, but this time we will add another player character into the mix, as well as locked scrolling as seen in classic side-scrolling shooter games.

We're ready to start our next game, a multiplayer side-scrolling shooter, but before we add any shooting, we'll need to have the multiplayer side-scroller part finished first. So let's get to it!

Time for action – creating the game assets and title screen

The first thing we will need to do is to create our game content and create the first layout of the game, the title screen.

1. First, draw up our player graphics and guns. We'll want the torso to be a separate object from the legs for easier animation. Use red dots where the legs will be attached to as markers for image point placement later on. Also include drawings for three weapons: a pistol, an uzi, and a shotgun:

2. Next, we can draw up our enemies for the game. In this case, we'll use an enemy robot with a turret arm that shoots balls of plasma:

3. We'll also need some scenery and ground objects for the levels:

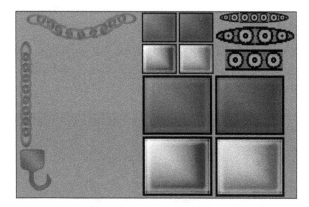

4. Finally, we'll need a graphic to tell the player to go onto the next screen when no enemies are present:

5. Now we can move on to starting our game. Create a new project and set its **Name** to SideShooter, and enter your **Creator** name. Then set the window size to 800 by 600.

6. Create the global variables CanGoNext, CurrentScreen, NumPlayers, P1Lives, P2Lives, GameWonLost, and RespawnY with values 0, 0, 1, 3, 3, 0, and 100 respectively.

7. Following that, rename the first layout to `Title` and its event sheet to `Title events`.

8. On this layout, create the layers `Text`, `Buttons`, and `Background` in top-to-bottom order.

9. Selecting the `Background` layer, create a `Panel` object and name it `Background` before setting its top corner filters to `Green` and bottom corner filters to `DarkGreen`. Stretch this object to cover the whole of the layout and lock the layer.

10. Now, on the `Buttons` layer, create a sprite and draw a box with the word `Play` in it.

11. Position this object in the center of the layout. This will be the start button for our game and should have the name `btnPlay`.

12. Next, add the `Mouse & Keyboard` and `XAudio2` objects into the layout and give them the global property.

13. In order to finish the layout design, create a `Text` object on the `Text` layer and set its name to `Title` and its text to `SideShooter`, and position it above the `btnPlay` object:

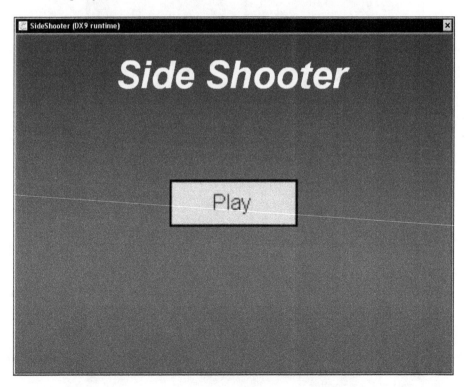

14. Switch over to the event sheet editor to add in a `Start of layout` event and use it to play a music file, `Title.mp3`, and loop it. This can be any title music you'd like, and it will also be played at the game's end screen.

15. Next, create an event for the `MouseKeyboard` object with the condition `Mouse is over object` to check if the mouse overlaps `btnPlay`.

16. Give this event the action `Set colour filter` for the `btnPlay` object to set the filter to `Grey - 40`.

17. Now create an `Else` event to set the filter color back to `White`.

18. In order to finish the event sheet, create an event with the condition `On object clicked` and select the object `btnPlay`.

19. Add actions to this event to set the value of `NumPlayers` to 1 and the value of `CurrentScreen` to 0 before adding the final `System` action `Next Layout`:

Time for action – designing the level

Now that we have our graphics created, we can put them into our second layout and make the first playable level.

1. Now we're ready to create a level layout. Create a layout and name it `Level1` and its event sheet `Level1 events`. Then create our main game event sheet `Game`.

2. For the layout, set its width to a multiple of the screen width (`800`), and check the box for **Unbounded scrolling**. In the event sheet of this layout, include our main event sheet `Game`.

3. Next, give this layout the layers HUD, Foreground, FrontScenery, Objects, LevelLights, ShadowCasters, BackScenery, and Walls in top-to-bottom order. After that, set the ScrollX and ScrollY rates of the HUD and Walls layers to 0%.

4. On the objects layer, create a Tiled Background object named Ground and give it the smaller light gray tile image. Ensure it has the Solid attribute and stretch and place some of them to form a level design.

5. Now create a Sprite object with the light green tile image and name it CrateBox. Give it the Solid attribute as well and place some around the level too. Have its collisions mode set to Bounding box.

6. Next, create a Sprite named ExitLevel and fill it with a solid color. Give it a width of 32 and stretch it so that it's taller than the display height (600). Then finish the object by checking the box for **Invisible on start** and placing it at the end of the level:

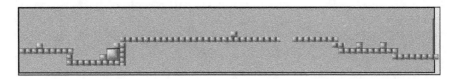

7. With the base layout complete, we can now add in three more invisible objects to handle scrolling. These are going to be Box objects with the names BackStopper, FrontStopper, and GoNextScreen.

8. Have the BackStopper and FrontStopper objects colored red and marked Solid with a width of 120.

9. Set the **Hotspot** property of the BackStopper object to Bottom-right, and the **FrontStopper** to Bottom-Left, before positioning them at 0,600 and 800,600 respectively.

10. Next, have the GoNextScreen box colored green and a width of 32 as well as a Hotspot of Bottom-right. Position this object at 800,600:

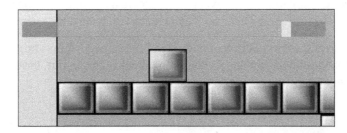

Time for action – creating player characters and conveyor belt objects

Now we can create our player character objects and also add moving and static conveyor belts into our level.

1. We are now ready to create our player objects. Start by inserting a Sprite and paste the standing image of the player character legs into it. Have an image point named 1 at the red spot that we drew earlier, and then place the hotspot at the bottom-middle point of the image (*num-pad 2*) as shown in the following image:

2. Name this sprite P1Legs, and for its Default animation, set the animation Tag to Stopped before checking the **Auto Mirror** checkbox in the main **Appearance** settings of the object.

3. Next, give it the platform behavior with the settings shown as follows:

Floor Acceleratior	1500
Floor Deceleratior	1500
Max floor speed	330
Air Acceleration	1500
Air Deceleration	1500
Max air speed	330
Max fall	1000
Jump strength	800
Jump sustain time	0
Fall Gravity	1500
Jump Gravity	1500
Jump Sustain Gra	0
Gravity Direction	Down
Inverse Control	☐
Allow bunny hop	☑
Allow down butt	☑
Auto Rotate	☑

4. Next, scroll down to the **Angle** properties box and check the **Auto mirror** checkbox.

5. Now we are ready to add the object to a family. Scroll up to the **Groups** sub-group **Families** and click on **Add** to bring up the **Construct: New Family** screen. Note that Construct Classic comes with some default families, but will also display any family that have been used previously:

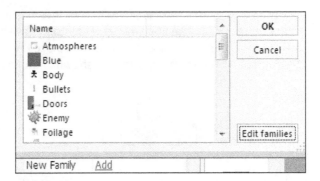

6. Click on **Edit Families** to bring up the **Construct: Families editor** screen. On this screen, enter the name **Legs** and click on the **+** button:

7. We can now draw the family image using the image editor that appears, shown as follows:

8. After finishing the image, save it by exiting out of the image editor and check that the family is now in the list. Once finished, click on **Done** to return to the family selection page.

9. Now select the **Legs** family and click on **Ok**:

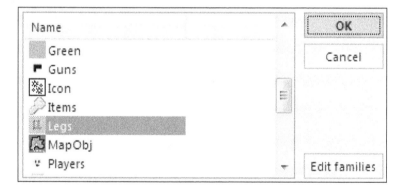

10. Now we can add the animation `Walk` in for our object. In this animation, set the `Tag` to `Walking`, and add the other leg sprites so they match the following image:

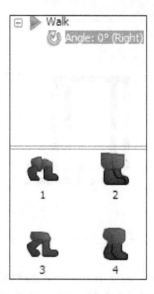

11. Now change the settings of the animation to have an **Animation** speed of 5 and check the **Loop** checkbox.

12. Next, copy the object and right-click on the layout to use the **Paste Clone** option, and name this clone as `P2Legs`. In the Platform behavior for this object, change the **Control** setting to `Player 2`.

13. Now go into the project properties and scroll to the bottom section, **Controls**. Click on the **Add / Edit** option for the **Manage Controls** setting at the bottom to bring up the controls box:

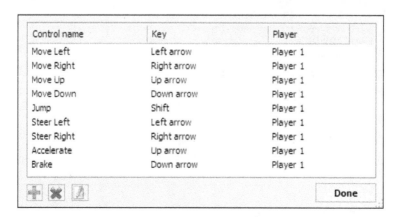

Control name	Key	Player
Move Left	Left arrow	Player 1
Move Right	Right arrow	Player 1
Move Up	Up arrow	Player 1
Move Down	Down arrow	Player 1
Jump	Shift	Player 1
Steer Left	Left arrow	Player 1
Steer Right	Right arrow	Player 1
Accelerate	Up arrow	Player 1
Brake	Down arrow	Player 1

Done

14. Use the `red X button` to remove all of the controls below `Jump`. Then click on the **Green plus** button to add a new control. Select this control and click on the **Pencil and paper** button to change its name to **Move Left**.

15. Click on the **Key** name for this control to bring up a drop-down box and set it to **A**.

16. Now, in the **Player** drop-down box, select **Player 2** for this control. It should match the following screenshot:

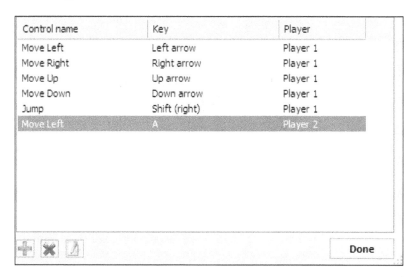

Control name	Key	Player
Move Left	Left arrow	Player 1
Move Right	Right arrow	Player 1
Move Up	Up arrow	Player 1
Move Down	Down arrow	Player 1
Jump	Shift (right)	Player 1
Move Left	A	Player 2

Done

17. Now continue to add controls until it matches the settings in the following screenshot before clicking on **Done**:

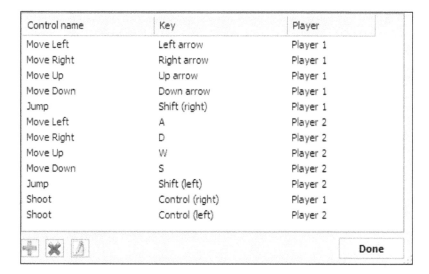

Control name	Key	Player
Move Left	Left arrow	Player 1
Move Right	Right arrow	Player 1
Move Up	Up arrow	Player 1
Move Down	Down arrow	Player 1
Jump	Shift (right)	Player 1
Move Left	A	Player 2
Move Right	D	Player 2
Move Up	W	Player 2
Move Down	S	Player 2
Jump	Shift (left)	Player 2
Shoot	Control (right)	Player 1
Shoot	Control (left)	Player 2

Done

18. Next, we'll create the bodies of our player objects. Create a `Sprite` called `P1Torso` and paste the normal body image of our character into it. Then position the `Hotspot` in the `bottom-middle` of the body. Give this sprite an image point 1 in the centre of its hand:

19. Rename the `Default` animation to `Normal` and set its speed to `0`, and check the **Auto Mirror** checkbox for this object as well.

20. Create two more animations, `Up` and `Down` respectively. Set their frames to match the following screenshot:

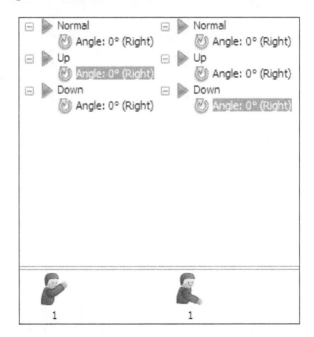

21. Now give the object a new family and name it `Body`. Then create `Private Variables` of names `Weapon`, `Ammo`, and `GunAngle`. Set the starting values to `0`, `99`, and `0` respectively.

22. Clone this object as well to create `P2Torso`, and replace the sprites with the second player graphics.

23. Now select `P1Legs` and scroll down to the **Groups | Container** properties to click on **Add object** and select **P1Torso**. The properties box and sprites should match the following screenshot:

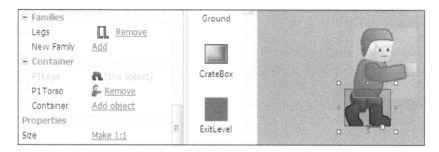

24. Next, put the `P2Torso` object into the container `P2Legs` using the same method.

25. Now, on the `Walls` layer, create a `Tiled Background` object named `FactoryWall` and paste the dark wall graphic into it. Then resize it to `800` in `Width` by `600` in `Height` and set its position to `0,0`. The layout should look similar to the following screenshot:

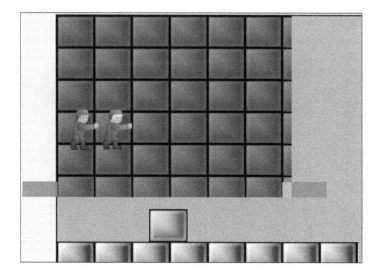

26. Switch to the `FrontScenery` layer and create a `Tiled Background` object called `ConveyorMiddle`, and give it the center piece of the conveyor belt images:

27. Give this object the `Private Variables` of `Direction` and `Speed` with starting values of `0`.

28. Place these around the map to act as scenery, as well as using them as an object to move players with at certain points. Set the `Direction` variable to `1` to have the conveyor belt move right, and `2` to move left. `Speed` is the attribute used to determine how fast a player character is moved by the conveyor belt; a speed of `25` works well in this instance. The following screenshot shows a moving conveyor belt in the layout:

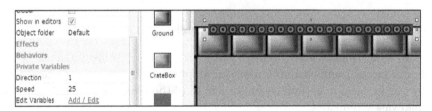

29. On the same layer, create a `Sprite` with the name `ConveyorStart` and `Collisions` set to `None`. Use the starting conveyor belt image for this object and set the `Hotspot` to the middle-right (*num-pad 6*). Give this sprite the `Attribute` of `Destroy on Startup`.

30. Create a second `Sprite` with the same settings called `ConveyorEnd` and a `Hotspot` in the middle-left (*num-pad 4*). Both sprites are shown in the following screenshot:

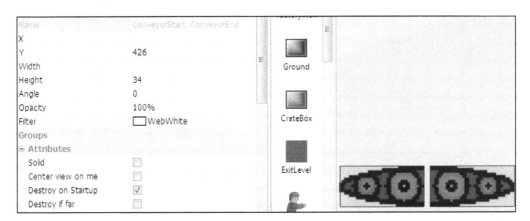

Time for action – creating the HUD objects

Now, we will move on to creating the Heads Up Display (HUD) objects for our game.

1. We are now ready to create the `HUD` objects for our game. Switch to the `HUD` layer and create a `Sprite` called `P1Face`, and give it an image of the `P1Torso` head and set its `Collisions` mode to `Bounding Box`:

2. Next, create a `Text` object called `P1Info` and set it up to match the following screenshot:

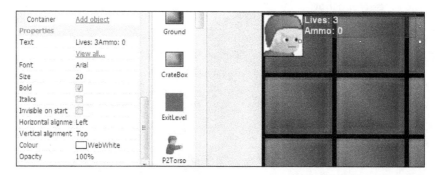

3. Create similar objects replacing `P1` with `P2` for the second player. In this case, have the objects match the following layout screenshot:

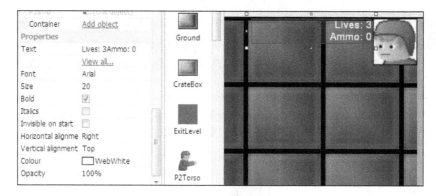

4. Now create a `Text` object for when the second player is not playing, and call it `P2Join`. Set its text to `Press left control to join` and have it matched to the following screenshot:

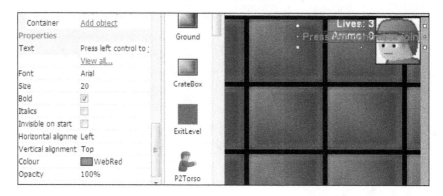

5. Give it a `Sine` behavior to make it fade in and out by matching its settings to those in the following screenshot:

Sine Behavior	
This behavior	⋀⋀ Remove
Name	Sine
Activate at start	☑
Movement	Opacity
Period	2000
Period Offset	0%
Range	100
Period Random	0
Period Offset Ranc	0%
Range Random	0

6. Now create the final `HUD` item, a `Sprite` called `NextSign`, and place the next arrow image into it. Set the `Collisions` of this object to `None`:

Time for action – creating the main game events

Now that our objects are set up, we can go on to make their events in the `Game` event sheet.

1. We are now ready to switch to the `Event Sheet Editor` to make the basics of our game. Start by adding an event sheet named `Game` to our project and include this from the event sheet of our level.

2. Open the `Game` event sheet and create the empty event groups `Startup`, `HUD`, `Scrolling`, `Enemies`, `Guns`, `Join-In`, `Players`, `Death`, `Sound`, and `LevelTransitions`. These can be given descriptions relative to their group name in their group creation dialog box:

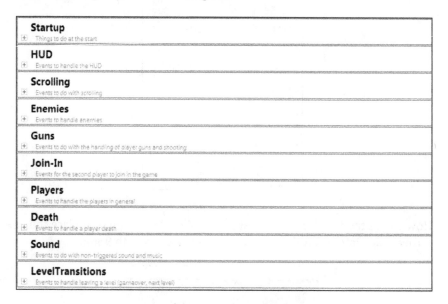

3. In the **Startup** group, add the `System` condition `Start of layout`. Add actions for the `BackStopper`, `FrontStopper`, and `GoNextScreen` objects to match those as shown in the following screenshot:

Startup
⊟ Things to do at the start

1	⊟ ⇨ Start of layout	☐ BackStopper: Set height to *LayoutHeight + 200*
		☐ BackStopper: Set X to *0*
		☐ BackStopper: Set Y to *LayoutHeight + 200*
		☐ BackStopper: Make **Invisible**
		☐ FrontStopper: Set height to *LayoutHeight + 200*
		☐ FrontStopper: Set X to *DisplayWidth*
		☐ FrontStopper: Set Y to *LayoutHeight + 200*
		☐ FrontStopper: Make **Invisible**
		☐ GoNextScreen: Set height to *LayoutHeight + 200*
		☐ GoNextScreen: Set X to *DisplayWidth*
		☐ GoNextScreen: Set Y to *LayoutHeight + 200*
		☐ GoNextScreen: Make **Invisible**

4. Now add actions to set the Global Variable values of GameWonLost and CurrentScreen to 0.

5. Next, add actions to destroy P2Legs and make P2Face and P2Info invisible, before finally adding actions to set the Global Variable values of P1Lives and P2Lives to 3. These actions should match those shown in the following screenshot:

6. Now add a sub-event with the For Each Object condition of the System object and select the ConveyorMiddle object.

7. Create a System object action Create object relative to object to spawn the ConveyorStart object on layer FrontScenery at 0, ConveyorMiddle. Height / 2 from the ConveyorMiddle object.

8. Do the same for the ConveyorEnd object, this time positioning it at ConveyorMiddle.Width, ConveyorMiddle.Height / 2 from the ConveyorMiddle object. The entire sub-event should now match the following screenshot:

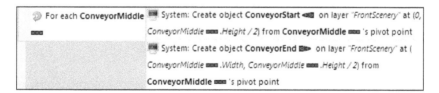

9. Now move to the HUD group and start here by creating an Always event to set the Text of P1Info to "Lives: " & global('P1Lives') & newline & "Ammo: " & P1Torso.Value('Ammo').

10. Add another event to this group to check if NumPlayers is 2. If so, then set the Text of P2Info to "Lives: " & global('P2Lives') & newline & "Ammo: " & P2Torso.Value('Ammo') and add an action to make P2Join set to Invisible.

11. Add an `Else` event just below the previous one to set the `P2Join` object to `Visible`. The three events should now look similar to the following screenshot:

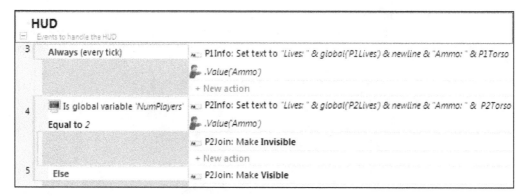

12. Now add an event to check if the variable `CanGoNext` is equal to `0` and give it an action to set the `NextSign` object to `Invisible`.

13. Add an `Else` event just below this and give it the additional condition `Every X Milliseconds` from the `System` object, and set its value to `250`.

14. Give this event a sub-event to check if **NextSign** is `Visible`, and give it an action to make it `Invisible`. Then add an `Else` event for this and have it make **NextSign** set to `Visible`, and play the sound `AppPath & "GoNext.wav"`:

15. Now move to the `Scrolling` event group, and add an `Always` event with actions to set positions of the `Body` family objects to the `Legs` family objects at image point 1. Then add another action to set the `Body` object `Angle` to `Legs.Angle`.

16. Now add the `System` object action `Scroll to X` to scroll to X position `BackStopper.X + (DisplayWidth / 2)`.

17. Now add an event to check when `Legs` is outside of the layout and `Invert` it. Give this event a further two sub-events, checking when `NumPlayers` is either equal to 1 or 2.

18. When `NumPlayers` is equal to 1, have an action to `Scroll to Y` of `P1Torso.Y`, but when it is equal to 2, have the game scroll to `((P1Torso.Y + P2Torso.Y) / 2)`. The two main event branches are shown in the following screenshot:

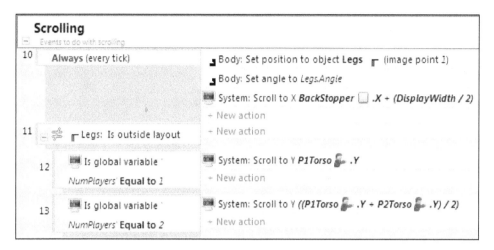

19. Add an event to check when the `X` of `Legs` is `Less or equal` to `BackStopper.X`. Give this event an action to set the `X` of `Legs` back to `BackStopper.X + (Legs.Width / 2)`.

20. Create an event for when the variable `CanGoNext` is equal to 1, and give it a sub-event that compares if `NumPlayers` is equal to 1 and a `Legs` object is overlapping the `GoNextScreen` object.

21. Add a second sub-event for the main event branch and have this compare when `NumPlayers` is equal to 2 and both `P1Legs` and `P2Legs` overlap the `GoNextScreen` object.

22. For both events, add actions to add 1 to CurrentScreen, and set the X positions of BackStopper, FrontStopper, and GoNextScreen to global('CurrentScreen') * DisplayWidth, (global('CurrentScreen') + 1) * DisplayWidth, and (global('CurrentScreen') + 1) * DisplayWidth respectively. The events should now look similar to the following screenshot:

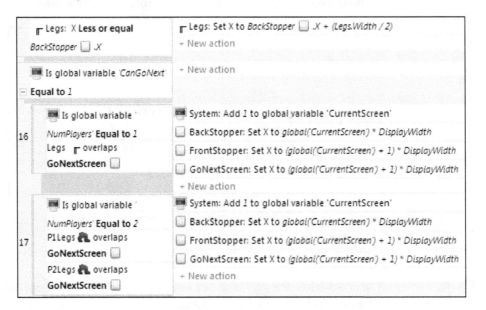

23. Now scroll down to the group Join-In and add an event with conditions to check when NumPlayers is equal to 1 and the control "Shoot" for player 2 is pressed for the MouseKeyboard object.

24. Give this event actions to set NumPlayers to 2 and create P2Legs on the "Objects" layer at X position (global('CurrentScreen') * DisplayWidth) + 50 and Y position global('RespawnY').

25. Finish the event by adding events to make P2Face and P2Info set to Visible:

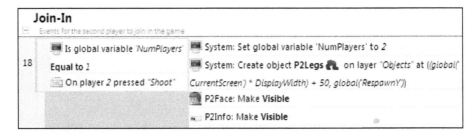

26. Move to the `Players` group and start with an `Always` event to send families `Legs` and `Body` to the front of their layout with the action `Send to front`.

27. Next, create an event for when the `Legs` family overlaps the `ConveyorMiddle` object.

28. Give this event sub-events to check when the `Private Variable` for `Direction` of the conveyor object is equal to `1` and when it is equal to `2`.

29. Using the action `Set X component of motion` for the `Platform` behavior of the `Legs` object, have the first sub-event set the value to `Legs[Platform].VectorX + ConveyorMiddle.Value('Speed')`, and for the second sub-event, set the value to `Legs[Platform].VectorX - ConveyorMiddle.Value('Speed')`:

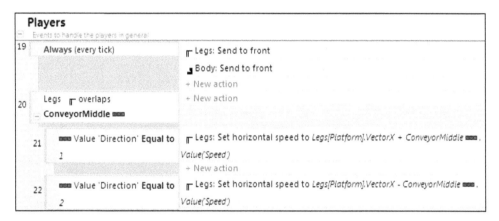

30. Now create an event for when the `Legs` object is overlapping the `Ground` object at an offset of `0, 20`. Have an action for this event to set the value of `RespawnY` to `Ground.Y - 250`.

31. Add events for both `P1Torso` and `P2Torso` with the condition `Control is down?` for the `MouseKeyboard` object to check when the control `"Move Up"` is down, or else `"Move Down"`, or an `Else` event for when neither is down. Give these events actions to set the animation of the torso object to `"Up"`, `"Down"`, and `"Normal"` respectively. The events should match the following screenshot:

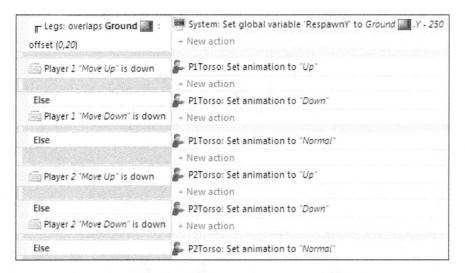

32. Scroll to the event group `Death` and create an event for when `P1Legs` is outside of the layout, and give it the additional condition `Trigger once while true`.

33. Add an action to this event to destroy `P1Legs` and another to play the sound `AppPath & "PlayerDie.wav"`.

34. Duplicate this event for `P2Legs`, but add an additional condition above the `Trigger once` condition to compare if `NumPlayers` is 2:

35. Now create an event to compare when P2Legs.Count is equal to 0, and give it the Trigger once condition.

36. Add a sub-event to check if P1Lives is greater than 0. Have an action to spawn the P1Legs object on the "Objects" layer at (global('CurrentScreen') * DisplayWidth) + 50, global('RespawnY') and a second to subtract 1 from P1Lives.

37. Next, create an Else event to set GameWonLost to 1.

38. Do the same for the P2Legs object and P2Lives variable. Above the Trigger once condition, add another condition to compare if NumPlayers is equal to 2. The two main events should match those shown in the following screenshot:

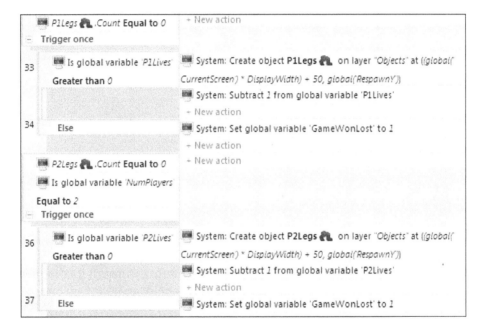

39. Scroll down further to the group Sound and add a Start of layout event to play the music file AppPath & "Game.mp3" and another to set it to Loop.

40. Add another event to check when ConveyorMiddle is on the screen and its Direction value is different than 0. Have a third condition to run the event every 500 milliseconds.

41. Create an action to play the sound AppPath & "Conveyor.wav" for this event.

42. Insert another event for when `Player 1` presses the control `"Jump"` and give it an action to play the sound `AppPath & "PlayerJump.wav"`. Have another event like this for `Player 2`, but also check that `NumPlayers` is equal to 2. All events in this group should now match the following screenshot:

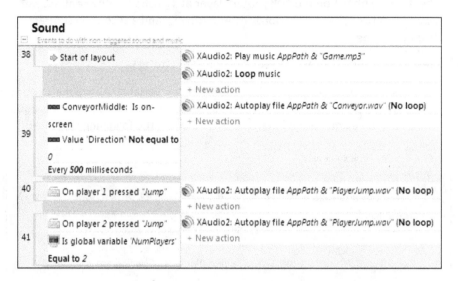

43. Now, in the final event group `LevelTransitions`, add an event for when `Legs` overlaps the `ExitLevel` object and `CanGoNext` is equal to 1. Have this event's action `GameWonLost` set to 2.

44. Next, add an event to destroy the `GoNextScreen` object when the `ExitLevel` object overlaps it.

45. Add a new event for when `GameWonLost` is equal to 1 and have it transition to the layout name `"GameOver"`. Then create an event when `GameWonLost` is equal to 2 to transition to the next layout.

Time for action – creating the Game Over layout

Our players also need a screen for when they lose or win the game, so let's make this layout now.

1. Now create the layout `GameOver` with layers `Text` and `Background` and its event sheet `GameOver Events`. Set this layout size to `800, 600`.

2. On the `Background` layer, create a `Panel` object stretched across the entire layout called `BackgroundRed` and set its color `Filter` to `WebRed`.

3. Next, on the `Text` layer, create three `Text` objects: `GameOver`, `GameSummary`, and `AnyKeyText` with the default text of `Game Over`, `You ran out of lives.`, and `Press any key to return to the title screen...` respectively:

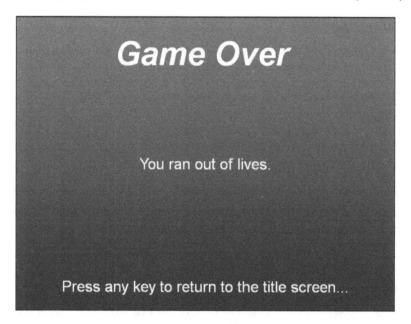

4. Switch to the `Event Sheet Editor` and add a `Start of layout` event to play the music file `AppPath & "Title.mp3"`, and set it to `Loop`.

5. Add sub-events to compare when `GameWonLost` is equal to 1 and another for when it is equal to 2.

6. In the first sub-event, add actions to set the text of `GameSummary` to `"You ran out of lives."` and the `Filter` of `BackgroundRed` to `WebRed`. For the second sub-event, set the text to `"Congratulations, you've completed the game!"` and set the `Filter` of `BackgroundRed` to `BrightGreen`.

7. In order to finish the event sheet, add an event for when any key is pressed and have it transition back to the layout "Title".

What just happened?

We've covered a large amount of ground in order to create the foundation of our third game, SideShooter. In between setting our game environment up, we managed to make a two-player game where the second player can join in at any time and players scroll by one screen at a time. Players can also get a "Game Over" from falling off the map, or be moved by conveyor belts.

Let us take a closer look at some of the things we've done.

Families

In this game, we used Families to consolidate the Torso and Legs objects of each player. This enabled us to create events for both of them by referencing their family rather than each object individually.

Containers

We used the Legs objects for containers of their respective Torso objects in order to have them spawn and be destroyed together. This also allows each Torso to know which pair of Legs to join to and allows us to spawn the second player character by only creating P2Legs.

Containers can be used in layout design to save the amount of objects being moved around. At startup, any objects in the layout that are part of a container will spawn their own counterparts automatically.

Multiplayer

Using the built-in controls system, we were able to add our own controls for the second player to use. Construct Classic behaviors will automatically use the controls generated by default and any controls with the same name for other players. Non-default controls such as Shoot must be checked from events, as we did for spawning the object P2Legs.

Static scrolling

We only allow the Y scrolling to be dynamically linked to the Y position of the players, but stop scrolling down when they fall off the screen.

For scrolling in the X axis, we used a mathematical formulae and the value of CurrentScreen to move by increments of the game screen width. Each time the players are able to continue and reach the end of a screen, we set the BackStopper object to the left edge of the new screen, and then the FrontStopper and GoNextScreen objects to the right edge.

Shooting bullets

Our players hold their hands out and aim up and down now, but they don't look right doing that without a gun in their hands.

We'll change this now by adding in guns, muzzle flashes, and bullets.

Time for action – adding some guns

Our players will need some tools to fight off any enemies we add later. Let us do this by adding in guns and bullets for them to use.

1. In the Layout Editor, select the Objects layer and create a sprite named PistolShot and paste the pistol bullet into it. Give this sprite the Attribute of Destroy on startup and a Private Variable named Damage with value 22.

2. Now set the Collisions mode to Bounding Box and add the object to a new family called Bullets.

3. Add the `Bullet` behavior and give it settings to match the following screenshot:

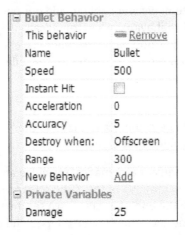

4. Clone this object and call it `UziShot`. Paste the uzi bullet image into it, set the `Damage` of this object to `20` instead, and have its `Bullet` settings match those shown in the following screenshot:

5. Do the same again for the `ShotgunShot` object, this time having a `Damage` of `18` and `Bullet` settings to match the following screenshot:

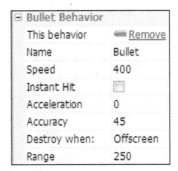

6. Now create a `Sprite` named `Pistol` and paste the pistol graphic into it. Have this object destroyed on startup and make it part of a new family `Guns`. Place image point 1 at the barrel of the gun.

7. Set the **Collisions** mode to `Bounding Box` and check the **Auto Mirror** checkbox before going on to add the `Private Variables` of `Player`, `WeaponNo`, and `CoolDown` with values `0`, `0`, and `500` respectively. Scale the gun to fit in the hand of the player torso objects, but also scale the `PistolShot` object to fit in its barrel.

8. Duplicate this object to make the `Uzi` and paste the uzi image into it. Set the `WeaponNo` to `1` and `CoolDown` to `250`. Scale this in the same way the `Pistol` object was scaled. Remember to readjust image point 1 to the new barrel.

9. Creating another duplicate, make an object called `Shotgun` and paste its respective image into it. Set the `WeaponNo` to `2` and the `CoolDown` to `1000` before scaling it to fit in a hand and scale the bullets it fires to the barrel. This object will also need the image point positioned at the barrel again.

10. Next, add another `Sprite` named `MuzzleFlash` and paste a white circle that fades to transparent into it. Set the size of it to `128`, `128`, the `Opacity` to `50%`, and `Filter` to a light shade of `yellow`. Check the **Attribute** checkbox of **Destroy on startup** and set the **Collisions** mode to `None`. Finish the object by adding the `Timer` behavior to it. All of the objects together should now match the following screenshot:

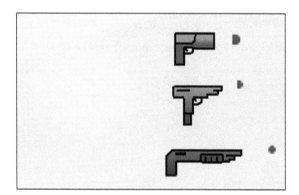

11. Switch to the `Event Sheet Editor` for the `Game` event sheet and scroll to the `Guns` event group.

12. Create a `For Each Object` event and select the `Bullets` object. Create two sub-events for when the `Bullets` family collides with the `CrateBox` object and the `Ground object`. Destroy the `Bullets` family object in each instance.

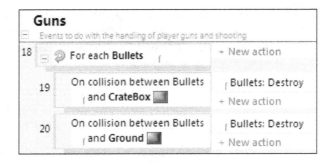

13. Now create a `For Each Object` event for the `Guns` object and give it the `Send to front` action for the `Guns` family of objects.

14. Next, add a sub-event for when the `Player` value of the `Guns` object is equal to `0`. Give the sub-event three further sub-events for when the value `WeaponNo` is equal to `0`, the `P1Torso` object collides with the `Guns` object, and the `P2Torso` object collides with the `Guns` object.

15. In the first sub-event, `Destroy` the `Guns` object. Then in the second, set `P1Torso` value `Weapon` to `Guns.Value('WeaponNo')`, the `P1Torso` value `Ammo` to `99`, and destroy the `Guns` object.

16. In the third sub-event, replicate the events from the second for the `P2Torso` object:

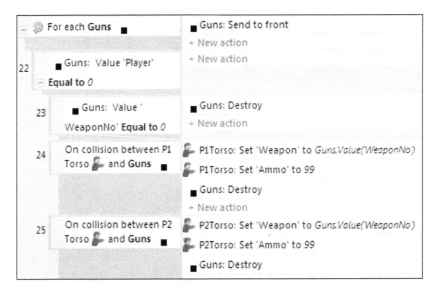

17. Next, add a sub-event to the For Each Object event again for when Guns value Player is equal to 1. Have an action to set the position of the Guns object to P1Torso at image point 1.

18. Give this event sub-events for when P1Torso animations "Up", "Down", and "Normal" are playing. Use these to set the P1Torso value of GunAngle to -40, 25, and 0 respectively.

19. Add another sub-event when the Angle of P1Torso is equal to 0 and have the Guns object set its Angle to P1Torso.Angle + P1Torso.Value('GunAngle').

20. Insert the next sub-event for when the Angle of P1Torso is equal to 180, and have an action to set the Guns object Angle to P1Torso.Angle - P1Torso. Value('GunAngle'). These events should all match the following screenshot:

21. Create another sub-event, this time for when player 1 holds down the control "Shoot", and give it an additional condition to run every Guns. Value('CoolDown') milliseconds.

22. Add actions to spawn the object MuzzleFlash on the Objects layer at image point 1 of the Guns object and then start timer "Flash" with a length of 50 and set to Destroy when finished. Have a third action to subtract 1 from P1Torso value Ammo.

23. Insert further sub-events to compare when `WeaponNo` of the `Guns` object is equal to 0, 1, or 2 and have a `Repeat 5 times` condition on the final sub-event as well.

24. For each of these sub-events, have the `Guns` object spawn the `PistolShot`, `UziShot`, or `ShotgunShot` objects respectively on the "Objects" layer at image point 1 and play the sounds `AppPath & "ShootPistol.wav"`, `AppPath & "ShootUzi.wav"`, and `AppPath & "ShootShotgun.wav"` respectively. The events will match the following screenshot:

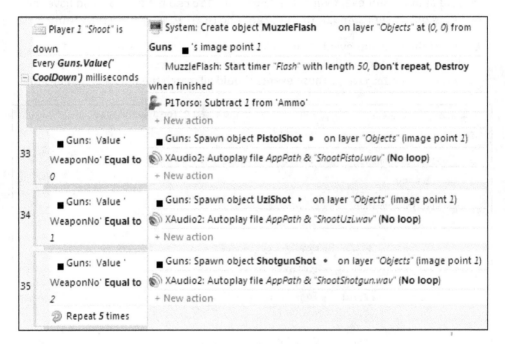

25. Duplicate the entire event structure for when `Guns` value `Player` is equal to 1 and replace each mention of 1 with 2. Add an additional condition to check `NumPlayers` is equal to 2 to the main branch of this, as shown in the following screenshot:

26. Now scroll to the `Players` event group below the event to compare `Body` value `Ammo` to being less than 0 and add an event to compare if `P1Torso` is equal to 99 and give it an additional `Trigger once` condition. Add a first sub-event to compare if the `Guns` value `Player` is equal to 1 and, if so, `Destroy` it.

27. Add another sub-event for when `P1Torso` value `Weapon` is equal to 0 and have it create a `Pistol` at image point 1 of `P1Torso` and set its value `Player` to 1. Give an additional action to set the `Ammo` of `P1Torso` to 0.

28. Create a similar sub-event, this time checking `Weapon` is equal to 1 and spawning an `Uzi` instead. Have the `P1Torso` value `Ammo` set to 30.

29. Add a final sub-event for when `Weapon` is equal to 2, and create the `Shotgun` object and set the `P1Torso` value `Ammo` to 15:

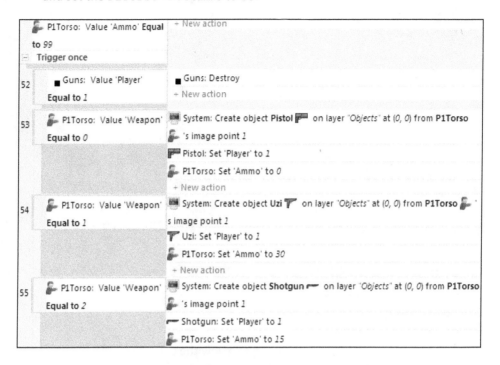

30. Finish this section of the chapter by repeating steps 1 through 30 for the `second player object` and having it also include a condition to check if `NumPlayers` is equal to 2 in the main event:

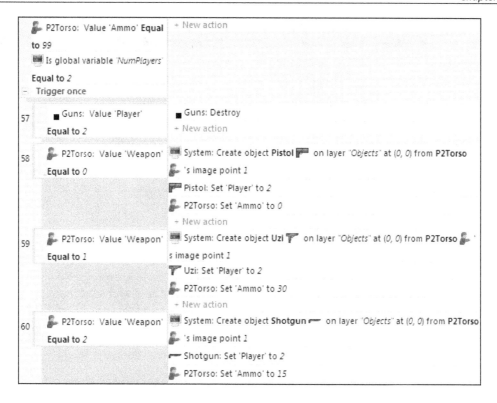

What just happened?

We now have guns that our players can pick up and shoot with muzzle flashes. By using the Spawn another object action for the Guns objects, we were able to create bullet projectiles for each type of Gun. The main bullets settings were controlled from the Bullet behavior of each, and once spawned, the bullets were able to keep moving on their own.

When changing weapons, we set the player Ammo value to 99 so the game knew that the player needed a new weapon.

Parallax: giving the impression of depth

Our game currently looks very flat. We can change this by creating parallax—layers that move at different speeds to appear as if they are different distances away from the player. Most side-scrolling games use this kind of effect to add atmosphere to levels.

Time for action – creating parallax scrolling

Luckily for us, Construct Classic makes parallax very easy with the scrolling rate values of each layer. Previously, we set these to 0% to stop scrolling completely for HUD layers, but now we can use it to add depth to our levels.

1. Change the Scroll X Rate and Scroll Y Rate values of the Foreground and BackScenery layers to 120%, 120% and 80%, 80% respectively.

2. On the Foreground layer, create a Sprite called StraightChain and paste in our vertical chain sprite. Size this up large and set its Collisions mode to None before placing a few copies of it along the map.

3. Create a similar Sprite named Hook with our hook sprite pasted into it at the ends of some of the chains.

4. Add a few more of these chain objects to the layers FrontScenery and BackScenery along the level. Remember that when the player sees them, they will be slightly offset to how they look in the Layout Editor.

5. Next, use the horizontal chain image to create the sprite HangingChain and have these hung from the ends of two or more straight chains along the level.

6. Finish designing the level by pasting the darker green crate image into a new sprite, CrateScenery, and have these objects on the BackScenery layer around the level. These scenery objects should look similar to those shown in the following screenshot:

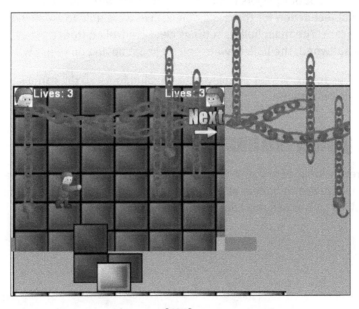

7. Now use `Run Layout` to see how the parallax effects appear in the game:

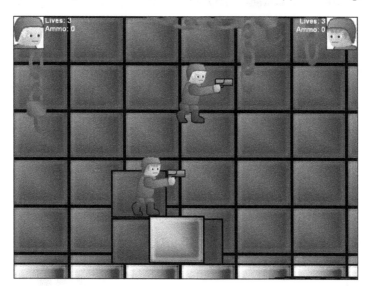

What just happened?

Without any events, we were able to add depth to our game by having objects on layers `Foreground` and `BackScenery` move with different speeds. Construct Classic can do many effects like this without any events, as we'll learn in the next chapter when we look at effects.

Have a go hero – add more scenery

Make this factory level more detailed by adding in further scenery objects in the `Foreground`, `FrontScenery`, and `BackScenery` layers.

Lights and shadows: illuminating the darkness

Our players seem to be walking around an empty factory rather than an abandoned one. Let us change this by adding a light to the layout and allow level objects to cast shadows. In order to do so, we'll now go on to learn how the built-in shadow and lighting engine of Construct Classic is used.

Time for action – using lights and shadow casters

Lighting and shadow engines are normally used in 3D games to add realism to the scene, but rarely they are also used in 2D games to improve visuals as well.

1. On the `LevelLights` layer, create a `Light` object called `WhiteLight` and accept the default image it comes with. Set its `Shadow filter` property to `WebBlack` and its `Shadow opacity` to 60%.

2. Place the object in your layout where you would like light to come in from:

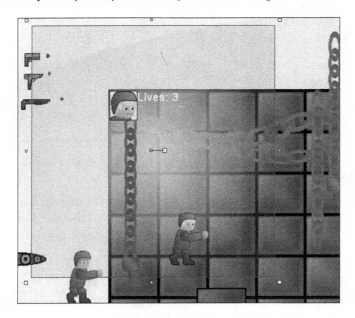

3. Now on the `ShadowCasters` layer, create a `Sprite` called `ShadowMask` and fill it with `Black`. Give this object the **Collisions** mode `None` and check the box for **Destroy on Startup** before adding the `Shadowcaster` behavior to it and setting **Shadow depth** to 1 and the shadow `Collision Mask` to `Bounding Box`.

4. Now switch over to the `Game` events, and in the `Startup` group add sub-events `For each Ground` object and `For each CrateBox` object to the main `Start of layout` event.

5. For the first sub-event, add actions to create the `ShadowMask` object on the `"ShadowCasters"` layer at `Ground.X + (Ground.Width / 2)`, `Ground.Y + (Ground.Height / 2)` and then set its size to `Ground.Width, Ground.Height`.

6. Do the same with the second sub-event, replacing `Ground` with `CrateBox`. The events should match those shown in the following screenshot:

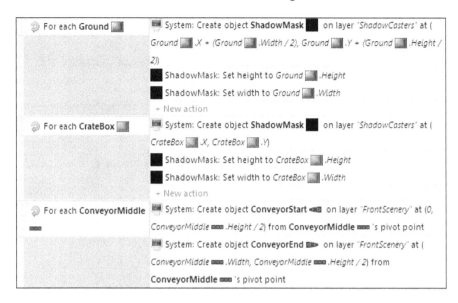

7. Now run the game to see the light and shadows in action!

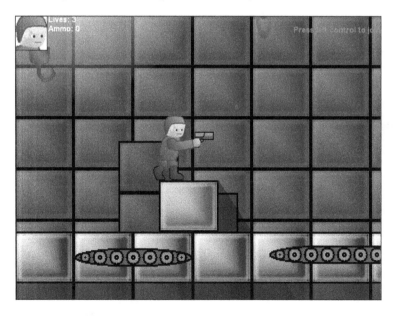

What just happened?

In a short time, we've learned how to add lights and shadow casters to our layout to use Construct Classic's built-in systems to create advanced effects. We used events on startup to automatically add a shadow caster object for each platform and crate in our levels.

Let us take a closer look at some of the variables, which we can use to change the appearance of our shadows:

- Shadow filter: This setting of the Light object lets us choose which color shadows will appear. This can be used to create strange effects such as a red fog to engulf the level.

- Shadow opacity: Lights can define how opaque shadows are. When set to 100%, no objects behind the shadows cast can be seen.

- Shadow Depth: This setting defines how far a shadow will stretch for. Usual values are decimals between 0 and 1.

- Collision Mask: Similar to the Physics engine, objects with the Shadowcaster behavior can have a manually drawn collision mask around them instead of the default Bounding Box.

Enemies with guns: slightly more challenging

Our players would be pretty bored if they were stuck on the same screen in the entire game with nothing to do. We will change this by adding in some enemies and give them basic AI to fight from afar with their guns, rather than fight like the aimless enemies we created in our first game.

Time for action – making some enemies

Players look for challenge and reason to play a game. Let us give our game one by adding in some enemy robots.

1. On the Objects layer of our layout, create a Sprite called SentryBot and paste our robot body into it. Place the hotspot of this object at its middle-bottom position (*num-pad 2*).

2. Set this object to Auto Mirror and scale it to being roughly shorter than the player objects. Add an image point 1 at the centre of the shoulder hole for the robot and add it to the family Enemy. Change the Rotation setting of the object to No rotation.

3. Next, create another sprite named TurretArm and paste in the robot's gun image. Change the Collisions mode to None and go back to the SentryBot object to add TurretArm into its container.

4. Now place multiple `SentryBot` objects around the level. Remember that the `TurretArm` objects are automatically created at runtime and do not need to be added in.

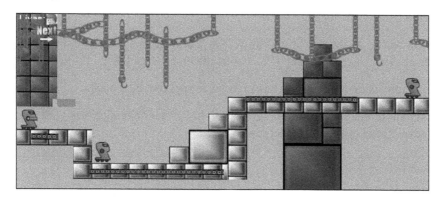

5. Create a `Sprite` called `EnemyFire` and paste the laser shot graphic into it. Give this object the `Attribute` of `Destroy on Startup` and a `Bounding Box` collisions mode. Next, add the `Bullet` behavior and set its values `Speed` to `500`, `Acceleration` to `-100`, `Accuracy` to `5`, and `Destroy when` to `Offscreen`.

6. Place the `hotspot` of this object at its front, but also insert an image point `1` for this object in its center.

7. Add in another `Sprite` with a white gradient image and name it `EnemyFireGlow`. Have this object keep its `WebWhite` filter and set its `Opacity` to `40%`, `Collisions` mode to `None`, and tick `Destroy on Startup`. Put this object into the container of `EnemyFire`:

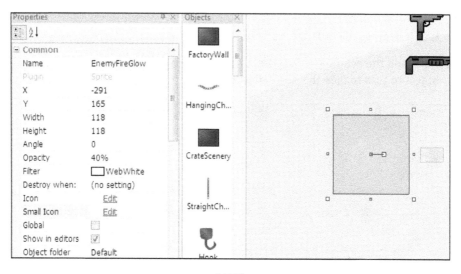

8. Now switch to the `Game` event sheet and scroll to the `Enemies` event group.

9. Start with an `Always` event to set the position of `EnemyFireGlow` to image point 1 on the `EnemyFire` object, and set the position of `TurretArm` to image point 1 of the `SentryBot` object.

10. Now add an event `For each SentryBot` and add a sub-event for when `SentryBot` is overlapping `"Solid"` at offset `0, 2` and `Invert` it.

11. Have an action to move the `SentryBot` at angle `90` by 6 pixels.

12. Add another sub-event for when `SentryBot` is overlapping a `"Solid"` and have it move 1 pixel at angle `270` degrees.

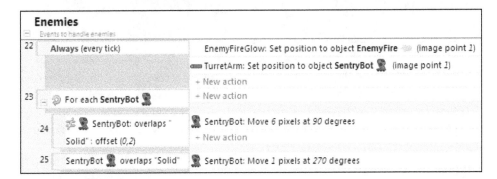

13. Now add another sub-event for when the `SentryBot` object is `on-screen`.

14. Give this sub-event a further sub-event for the `Body` family with the condition `Pick closest` and enter the position of `SentryBot.X, SentryBot.Y`.

15. Add the action `Rotate towards another object` for the `TurretArm` object to turn 3 degrees towards the `Body` object.

16. Next, add the action `Set angle towards another object` for the `SentryBot` object to turn to face the `Body` object:

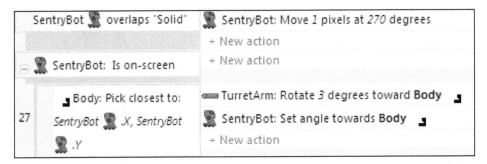

17. This sub-event will then have three sub-events below it. For the first, add conditions to compare if `anglediff(TurretArm.Angle, angle(TurretArm.X, TurretArm.Y, Body.X, Body.Y))` is lower than `40` and only trigger `Every 1500 milliseconds`. Create actions for the `TurretArm` object to spawn the object `EnemyFire` on layer `"Objects"` from image point `1` and send `TurretArm` to the front of the layer before playing the sound `AppPath & "SentryShoot.wav"`.

18. The second sub-event should have a condition to check if `SentryBot.X` is greater than `Body.X` and inverted conditions checking that `SentryBot` is overlapping `"Solid"` at `-60,0` and overlapping `Body` at `-60,0`. Create an action to move the `SentryBot` by `2` pixels at `180` degrees.

19. For the third sub-event, add similar conditions checking that `SentryBot.X` is lower than or equal to `Body.X` and check for collisions at offset `60, 0`. Have the action move the `SentryBot` by `2` pixels at `0` degrees instead. These events should match the following screenshot:

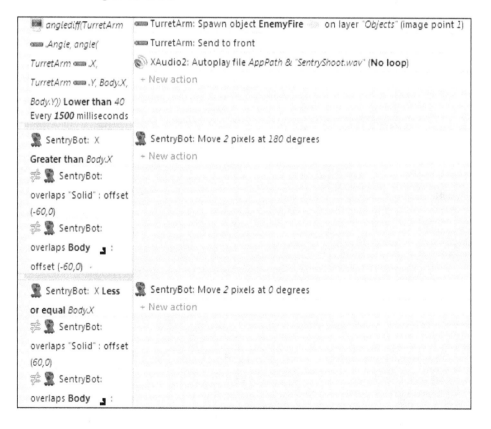

20. Now, outside of all the sub-events, add an event for when `EnemyFire` collides with `"Solid"` objects and add an action to `Destroy` the `EnemyFire` object.

21. Next, add an event `For each Enemy` object and a sub-event for when `Enemy` value `HP` is less or equal to `0` and have it `Destroy` the `Enemy` object.

22. Add another sub-event below to compare if `random(3)` is equal to `2` and have it create a `Guns` object on the layer `"Objects"` at `0, (Enemy.Height / 2) * -1` from the `Enemy` object:

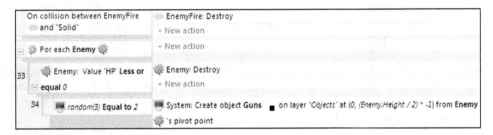

23. Scroll to the `Guns` event group, and in the `For each Bullets` event, add a sub-event for when `Bullets` collides with `Enemy`.

24. Create an action to `Flash` the `Enemy` object for a `0.1` second interval and `1` second of flashing.

25. Next, add actions to subtract `Bullets.Value('Damage')` from `Enemy` value `HP` and `Destroy` the `Bullets` object before playing the sound `AppPath & "EnemyHit.wav"`.

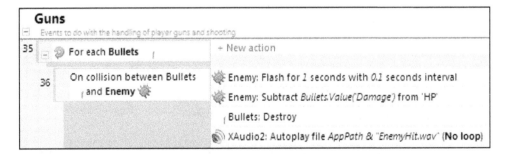

26. Now, scroll to the `Death` event group and add a new event with conditions `Collision between P1Torso and EnemyFire`, `OR`, and `Collision between P1Legs and EnemyFire`.

27. Insert actions to `Destroy the P1Legs` object and `EnemyFire` object and play the sound `AppPath & "PlayerDie.wav"`.

28. Duplicate this event for `P2Torso` and `P2Legs` to finish the events for this chapter:

29. Now, export and try playing through your game with a friend!

What just happened?

We have now finished the first part of our game—`SideShooter`—by adding in enemies that shoot back at the players and move towards them when they can.

Here's a closer look at some of the things we've just done.

Manual collision detection

Instead of using behaviors, we used simple events to check when the SentryBot object is overlapping a "Solid" object. Our first event moves the SentryBot down when it is not above a solid object, while the second event will move the SentryBot back up if it moves down too far.

Basic AI

We only activated enemy AI when they were on-screen to prevent every enemy in the level moving onto the first screen. We then used the expression AngleDiff to compare the angle between the TurretArm object and the Body object. When this angle was less than 40, the TurretArm was pointed close enough to the player to fire, rather than constantly firing in any direction and reducing the intelligent appearance of our enemies.

We then added two more events for moving the SentryBot object towards the player when it was not overlapping any "Solid" object and did not stand in the same spot as the player.

Spawning a gun

When an enemy dies, the player has a 1/3 chance of a Guns object spawning randomly. This object will automatically be one of the three objects in its family without any further events needed.

Pop quiz – a shot in the dark

Let us try a multiple choice pop quiz to see how much we remember of the chapter.

1. In order to use the built-in shadow engine, what objects are needed in a layout?

    a. A Light object only

    b. A Light and Shadow object

    c. A Light object and an object with the Shadow Caster behavior

2. Which is true about shadows?

    a. They can only be shades of black

    b. They can overlap and darken other shadows

    c. They overlap all objects in a layout

3. How is a bullet fired by a `Sprite`?

    a. By using the Sprite action `Spawn another object` to shoot the `Bullet`

    b. By creating a `Bullet` object and using its action `Fire`

    c. By using `Sprite` action `Spawn another object` to create the `Bullet` and then use its action `Fire`.

Summary

We've now finished the first and largest part of our third game. In this chapter, we created the beginnings of our side-scrolling shooter game complete with multiplayer and enemies.

We first took steps for making the game multiplayer using Construct Classic's built-in control system to allow a second player to play alongside the main character. Next, we learned how to add guns and bullets into our games. We added a `Pistol`, `Uzi`, and `Shotgun` into our game with different behaviors between them.

Our next steps then involved creating parallax effects to give depth to our level scenery, and adding lights and shadows to our game with the built-in systems of Construct Classic. Finally, we created a new kind of enemy, which hunts the player(s) and is able to shoot back at them.

Now that we have a fully playable game, we can go on to learn how to add special weapons, such as grenades, and use pixel shader effects in Construct Classic, which is covered in our next chapter.

8
I'm Throwing a Grenade!

In the last chapter, we learned how to create our first multiplayer 2D platform shooter game. We're ready to learn one of the final parts of making games with Construct Classic—the special effects.

In this chapter, we will:

◆ Learn how to create an exploding, bouncing grenade object in our game

◆ Learn how to use effects to distort the screen when the grenade explodes

◆ Learn how to fire our enemies away from a grenade blast

So let's get on with it.

Grenades – bouncing, timed explosives

Our players may need a helping hand when they're trying to fight the enemy robots. To do so, we'll be adding in the secondary weapon of grenades, which they'll be given at the start of each level and can be thrown by pressing their *Jump* and *Shoot* keys at the same time.

Time for action – throwing grenades

We're now ready to add a grenade object into our game for the players to use in their quest to destroy the robot factory.

1. Draw up a grenade object image to use in the game that resembles the one shown in the following image:

2. Add a sprite to the Objects layer of our game. Give this sprite the name Grenade and paste the image into it.

3. Give the Grenade object the Physics behavior and the settings shown in the following screenshot:

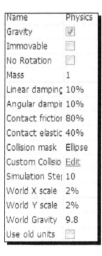

Name	Physics
Gravity	☑
Immovable	☐
No Rotation	☐
Mass	1
Linear damping	10%
Angular damping	10%
Contact friction	80%
Contact elastic	40%
Collision mask	Ellipse
Custom Collision	Edit
Simulation Step	10
World X scale	2%
World Y scale	2%
World Gravity	9.8
Use old units	☐

4. Give the object the Timer behavior to add countdown timers to the object as needed with events.

5. Check the attribute **Destroy on Startup** before finally setting the Collisions mode to Bounding box.

6. Create two more `Global Variables`, `P1Grenades`, and `P2Grenades` respectively.

7. We can now go into the **Event Sheet Editor** for the `Game` event sheet to create the events to control `Grenades`.

8. In our `Start of layout` event, add actions to set the variables `P1Grenades` and `P2Grenades` to `3`.

9. Create an event group `Grenades` with a `Description` of `Events to deal with Grenades` and add an `Always` event to it.

10. Give this event the action `Send to front` for the `Grenade` object.

11. Create an event with the `MouseKeyboard` condition **Control is down?** to check if player `1` is pressing `"Shoot"`. Add the same condition again, but checking for `"Jump"`.

12. Add a condition to check if the global variable `P1Grenades` is `Greater than` the value `0`, and another condition to check if the value of `Grenade.Count` is `Equal to` the value `0`.

13. We are ready to add actions to the event. Start by adding a `Spawn another object` action for the `P1Torso` object, and create the `Grenade` object on the `"Objects"` layer at image point `1`.

14. Following that, add the `Set torque` action for the `Physics` behavior of the `Grenade` object to set its torque to `2`.

15. Add another action for the `Grenade` object. This time, choose the `Physics` behavior action `Add force towards position` and set the **X co-ordinate** to `P1Legs.X`, the **Y co-ordinate** to `P1Legs.Y - 20`, and the **Force** to `-70`.

16. Add a `Timer` action for the `Grenade` to start the timer `"Explode"` with a length of `3000 + random(500)` and not to repeat or destroy the object.

17. To finish the event, add an action to subtract `1` from the global variable `P1Grenades`.

18. Clone this event and replace the references to player 1 with player 2. The events so far should match the following screenshot:

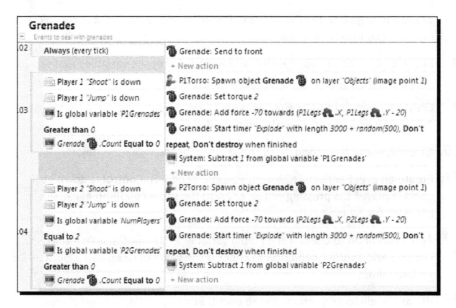

19. Add an event for when the `Grenade` collides with the `FrontStopper` object. Add a `System` condition `OR` to also run the event when the `Grenade` collides with the `BackStopper` object.

20. Create the action `Add force` for the `Physics` behavior of the `Grenade` object to set the **X component** of the force to `(Grenade[Physics].VelocityX * -1) * 23` and its **Y component** to `0`.

21. Create an event for when the `Grenade` object collides with a `Ground` object.

22. Following that, create a sub-event `Compare Y position` for the `Grenade` object to check if it is less than `Ground.Y`.

23. Give this sub-event the action `Add force` for the `Grenade` object, and set its **X component** to `0` and **Y component** to `(Grenade[Physics].VelocityY * -1) * 23`.

24. Add an `Else` sub-event below the initial collision event. Create another `Add force` action, this time with the **X component** of `(Grenade[Physics].VelocityX * -1) * 23` and **Y component** of `0`. These events should match the following screenshot:

25. Add an event to check when the `Grenade` object collides with a `CrateBox` object. Add a sub-event for when the **Y** of the `Grenade` object is `Greater or equal` to `CrateBox.Y - (CrateBox.Height / 2)`.

26. For this sub-event, create another `Add force` action for the `Grenade`, this time with **X component** of `(Grenade[Physics].VelocityX * -1) * 23` and **Y component** of `(Grenade[Physics].VelocityY * -1) * 23`.

27. Create an `Else` sub-event to add a force of **X component** value `0` and **Y component** value `(Grenade[Physics].VelocityY * -1) * 23` to the `Grenade` object.

28. Add an event for the `Grenade` object with the `Timer` behavior condition `On timer` to check when `"Explode"` ends. Create an action to `Destroy` the `Grenade` object.

29. Create a sound effect for the explosion and name it `GrenadeExplode.wav` before putting it in the games directory.

30. Add an action to play the sound `AppPath & "GrenadeExplode.wav"`. The events we just created should now match following screenshot:

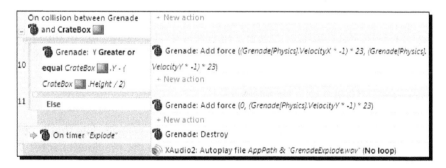

What just happened?

We've now created our Grenade object, and when we run our game, the players can throw a grenade that slows down and eventually disappears with the sound of an explosion.

Let us take a look at how we did it.

Throwing the grenade

We created it so that the player's character can throw a grenade when both controls are pressed simultaneously. We also ran a check that no other grenades were being thrown, and that the player had enough grenades left to throw.

We then had the grenade thrown at an angle from the player's character by adding a force away from the mid-point of the character's base.

Bouncing the grenades

Rather than adding the Physics behavior to all of our objects, we created events to check for collisions between the grenade and the scenery to make it bounce correctly. Friction was handled by the physics engine for us, so bouncing was all we worried about. We used -1 to flip the components of velocity, and then multiplied by 23 to increase the force so the grenade bounces back into the air.

For bouncing off borders, we simply reversed the X component of the grenade's movement, but for the ground we needed to bounce it differently when it was above or below its top. When it was above the ground, we simply reversed its Y component, but when it was below the ground, the Else sub-event triggered and the grenade was bounced sideways by flipping the X component of motion.

We also checked for when the Grenade collides with the CrateBox object. As the hotspot of the CrateBox object is at its midpoint, we used CrateBox.Y - (CrateBox.Height / 2) to calculate the top Y position. When the grenade is below the top of the crate, we bounced it both in the X and Y components, but when it is above, we just bounce it upwards.

Explosions – big bright lights

Right now, our grenades disappear when the timer runs out. Let's change that by giving them a yellow glow similar to the muzzle flash we created in the previous chapter. We'll use this object to show the blast of the explosion.

Time for action – explosion flashes

We have a grenade that explodes, but produces no flash. So let's add this in now.

1. In the **Layout Editor** view, create a layer called `Effects` and place it just behind the `HUD` layer.

2. Add a `Sprite` with the name `GrenadeExplosion` and a more solid circle version of the `Light` object image (a quick way of doing this is to paste the sprite in multiple times; each time decreases the opacity).

3. Set the hotspot of the `Sprite` to its mid-point (*numpad 5*).

4. Set the `Opacity` value to `40%` and `Filter` to `WebYellow`, then give it the `Timer` behavior. The object should now look similar to the image in the following screenshot:

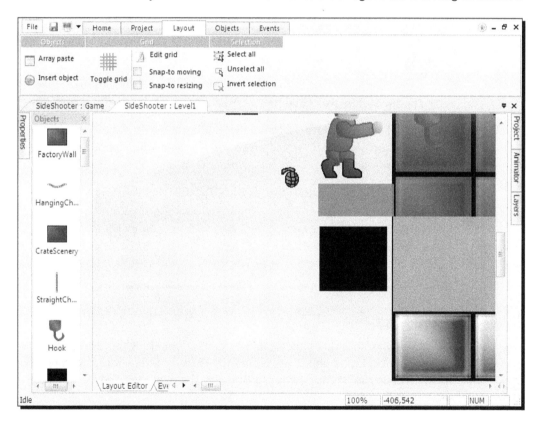

5. Switch over to the **Event Sheet Editor** view. In the event where the Grenade object explodes, add an action at the top of the list to spawn the GrenadeExplosion at the position of the Grenade object on the "Effects" layer.

6. Add an action to start the Timer behavior of the GrenadeExplosion object with the name "FlashTimeout" of length 100 and Destroy the object when the timer ends. The event should match the following screenshot:

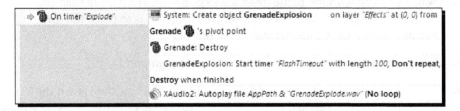

7. In order to make the enemies get damaged by the explosion, scroll up to the Enemies event group, and under the SentryBot: Is on-screen sub-event, add a System event Compare to check if distance(SentryBot.X, SentryBot.Y, GrenadeExplosion.X, GrenadeExplosion.Y) is Lower than the value 300.

8. Add a **Trigger once while true** condition into the event.

9. To finish, add actions to remove 30 from the health of the SentryBot, cause the enemy to flash, and play the hit sound as we had it played when hit by bullets. The event should now look similar to the following screenshot:

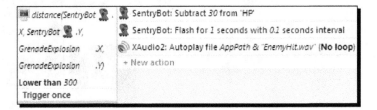

What just happened?

We now have an explosion radius that appears and damages enemies within 300 pixels. We made it in a way that the explosion object will destroy itself using a timer. At the completion of this topic, we also set up the Effects layer for showing the explosion and using it later on for distortions. These steps have prepared us for the next sections.

Effects – distortions and other nice things

Our grenade now bounces and explodes with a flash, but we'll add a distortion effect to add a nice look to the explosions, while we also learn how to use effects in Construct Classic.

Time for action – adding some distortion

We are now ready to add in a small distortion effect to the explosion of our grenades. This will provide a nice visual for players and teach us the basics of using effects.

1. On the `Effects` layer, create a `Sprite` in the same way we created the `GrenadeExplosion` image, and then name it `ExplosionDistort` and size it to `32` by `32`.

2. In the `Effects` group of the objects properties, click on **Add** and select the **Distort Normal** effect to add it to our object, as shown in the following screenshot. The object will now appear invisible, but magnify any objects it overlaps.

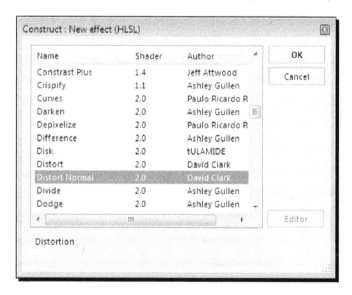

3. Now add another effect called `Warp`, and have the two set up to match the following screenshot:

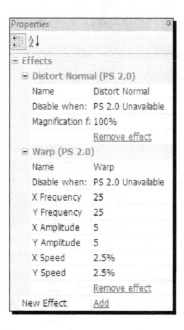

4. Set both the `GrenadeExplosion` and `ExplosionDistort` objects to be destroyed on startup, and switch over to the **Event Sheet Editor**.

5. In the `Grenades` event group `Always` event, add actions to set the `Height` of `ExplosionDistort` by `ExplosionDistort.Height + 24`, and the `Width` to `ExplosionDistort.Width + 24`. This event should now match those shown in the following screenshot:

6. Scroll down and create an action to create the object `ExplosionDistort` on the `"Effects"` layer at the position of the `Grenade` object when its `"Explode"` timer ends.

7. Finally, add an event with conditions **Compare width** and **Compare height** for the `ExplosionDistort` object to check when they are over `512`. Give this event an action to destroy the `ExplosionDistort` object. The events should look similar to the following screenshot:

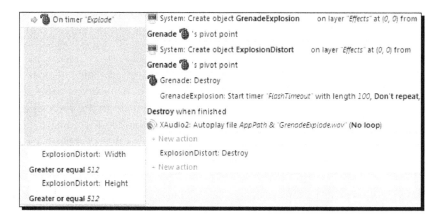

What just happened?

When the game is run, we now see a magnifying distortion when a grenade explodes. To do this, we created a simple sprite object and attached pre-made effects to it. We saw that effects can be combined as we saw with the `Warp` and `Distort Normal`, where one caused the sprite to change shape and the other magnified objects in the background.

Now let's see what we did in some more detail.

Pixel shaders

We added effects from a simple list and then changed their default settings from the Properties box. We noticed that both of our effects used, mention they are `PS 2.0`. This tells us that a graphics card with support for **Pixel shader version 2** or later is required for the effect to work. This is why we set the `Disable when:` option to stop the effect when the graphics card doesn't support it.

You may have noticed an option to disable effects when the pixel shader is available. This is actually to allow an object to swap between effects when different levels of pixel shader become available. This can be used to save objects and events when planning to run on different computer hardware.

The effects used

We used the effect `Distort Normal` to magnify objects in the background with strength according to how transparent the sprite image is for each pixel. This means the center of our sprite received the greatest amount of magnification, while the outer edges received none. However, to make it look like there were heated gases moving rather than a simple magnifying glass, we used the `Warp` effect to distort the image of the sprite. It had settings to change the speed and size of the distortion in both vertical and horizontal directions.

Effects can be combined in many ways to produce interesting effects, but the documentation on them is usually very limited. In most cases, you will need to experiment to get the outcome you're looking for. Or, if you know exactly what you want to do, you can code your own effects in **High Level Shader Language** (**HLSL**) and save them in the Construct effects folder. Many users on the Scirra forums have posted their own effects for download, ready to be put to use in whatever games need their help.

Have a go hero – more visual effects

Now that we've learned how to add effects to objects, try out some of the others to see what they do, and improve the overall effects quality in your game.

Another way to improve the visuals of our game is to add in particle effects for the explosion, or create fading smoke particles when the explosion is gone. To do this, remember to tick the `One-shot` property in this case, as it will destroy the `Particles` object after it creates its first batch of particles.

Objects – completely blown away

We want to blast any robots caught by the blast out of the way, but we don't want them to be blasted into the ground or walls. So in this section, we'll learn how to move them away from the blast with a small set of events.

Time for action – blast the robots away

Our `SentryBot` enemies get hurt by grenades, but let's have them pushed away from the explosion as well. In this section, we'll perform a simple position comparison to move them in the right direction, and then use our existing collision events to push them out of whatever objects they may end up stuck in.

1. In the event where we damage the `SentryBot` from a collision with the `GrenadeExplosion` object, add a sub-event to check if `SentryBot.X` is Lower than the value of `GrenadeExplosion.X`.

2. Give this sub-event the `SentryBot` action `Move at angle` to move 80 pixels at 180 degrees.

3. Finally, create another sub-event for when the opposite case occurs, and move the `SentryBot` by 80 pixels at 0 degrees. The event should match the following screenshot:

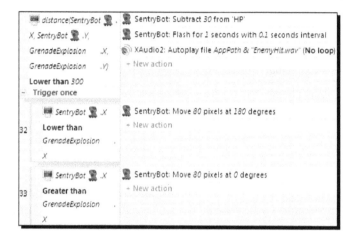

What just happened?

To finish off our game, we used a simple set of events to move the `SentryBot` to the left or right of the explosion, as we had already put events in place to move the object out of the ground and crate objects. Now, we can export the game and share it with friends and family.

Have a go hero – extend the game

We've now finished learning how to make our third game, but it's only one level so far. Try adding a whole campaign of levels, and see how you and a friend do at getting through it.

Pop quiz – looking back on timers and effects

Let's try a multiple choice pop quiz to see how much we remember of the chapter.

1. What is the `Timer` behavior used for?

   a. To add a single timer countdown to an object

   b. To call timer countdowns via events for an object

   c. To display a visual timer clock for the object

2. What is true about `Effects` in Construct Classic?

    a. They will not work on a computer with a Pixel Shader model lower than stated as a requirement

    b. They can slow a game down if too many are used at once

    c. They are attached directly to objects or layers

    d. All of the above

3. What do `Effects` change in an object?

    a. Effects change how a `behavior` controls the object

    b. Effects change the image of an object in the `Layout Editor`

    c. Effects change how an object is displayed at runtime

Summary

In this chapter, we've finished our third and final game by adding grenades that throw enemies around and explode with a warping distortion effect. We first learned to create bouncing grenades using events to control the `Physics` behavior when colliding with regular sprites. This required manually checking for collisions, but another way to do this would be to add the `Physics` behavior to all objects that the `Grenade` is to collide with.

We then learned how to create an explosion flash similar to the muzzle flashes when bullets are fired. To complete the visual imagery, we went on to adding effects into the game such as distortions and warping sprites.

We explored how to move objects away from each other with events, before we finally discussed extending our game by adding additional levels, enemies, and effects.

Now that we've created our three games, we're ready to learn some additional features of Construct Classic that we haven't got to use yet and reflect on important things we've learned so far, which is what we look at in the next chapter.

9
Our Final Moments

We've now reached the final chapter of this book, but we still have some final things to learn before we depart. In this chapter, we'll see the core skills we've learned in Construct Classic, and then go on to learning smaller skills we may need in future games.

In this chapter, we shall:

- ◆ Take a look at everything we've learned
- ◆ Look ahead to where we can go with our games
- ◆ Learn some final tips and tricks to use in our future games

So let's get on with it.

What we've learned

Things really sped up as we came to making our last game. Let's slow down to look at all the things we've learned throughout the book.

Chapter 1, the basics of the Construct Classic editor

We started our journey by learning our way around the Construct Classic editor. This let us move into the future topics quickly while also introducing us to the main game object type, the `Sprite`.

Chapter 2, our first game, MyPlatformer

After learning the basics of the editor, we were able to learn the skills necessary to make a simple starter game, `MyPlatformer`. This chapter taught us more about using sprites as game objects, as well as using `Tiled Backgrounds` to make up the levels. To make the game possible, we were then introduced to behaviors, private variables, textboxes, and finally we created events for the game.

Chapter 3, adding enemies and a lives system

This chapter taught us how to add a challenge to our game by guiding us through the creation of enemies and a lives system, to make the player lose the entire game after three failed attempts.

Two important skills we learned were controlling the movement of the enemy sprites from events and creating static layers that can be used for displaying information to the player, but doesn't move with the rest of the game.

Chapter 4, playing sounds and music

In this chapter, we were able to learn the skills necessary to play various formats of music and sound files in our game. We used these skills in every game we've made in this book and will most likely be using it in all our future games as well.

Chapter 5, a physics game

Moving on to more complex features of Construct Classic, we created `BounceBall`, a physics-based puzzle game to learn how to use the physics engine, while also learning how to use event sheets to save us from re-writing events throughout layouts, which we also learned to transition between.

This chapter finally taught us how to see the finer details of what happens in our games by using the debugger.

Chapter 6, custom levels and level editors

In this chapter, we learned about the INI file and how we can use them to store level information. These files can be used for all kinds of data from maps to game dialog and even for customizing game objects.

We used our new knowledge of using INI files to create a level editor for our game so players can enjoy their own custom levels, as well as making level editing easier for ourselves.

Most big games need level editors, even if they are never released. They save time in level design and allow multiple developers to work simultaneously on content for the game. Construct Classic does not allow copying between projects without having bugs or even crashing entirely. As such, making your game import its data is the best way for letting multiple people work on it at once.

Chapter 7, A sidescrolling shooter

We started our final game, SideShooter, in this chapter to learn how to add multiple player characters, fire projectiles, create illusions of depth with parallax, use Construct Classic's lighting and shadow engine, and create enemies with guns to retaliate as well.

Multiplayer games can also be achieved by using events to entirely move objects or control their behaviors. But in most cases, the built-in movement behaviors work well for the standard game designs.

Chapter 8, effects and physics interactions

To finish the last game of the book, we went on to add grenades to our game and learned how to use Construct Classic's powerful pixel shader effects to render a distortion when they explode.

We also learned what is necessary to perform simple collisions between physics objects and non-physics objects from events. As the physics behavior tries to move all objects that use it by default, we can use such events to avoid adding behavior to objects that already have other movement behavior.

Extending our games

We have now finished all of our three games. Let's take a look at what we can add to each of the three games that we didn't get to add when we made them.

MyPlatformer

We started very simple with this game, with no title and game over or victory screen. We can extend this game by adding some more levels and adding more enemy types for the player to face.

We can also make the levels more interesting by adding parallax scenery as well as moving platforms for the player to travel with. An easy way to do the latter is to have the platform move between two sprites, but there is also a free Path Movement plugin on the Scirra forums that can be used.

BounceBall

This game is almost complete, with the only elements missing being the additional content and levels. Try adding settings to the INI file for playing different songs on each level, and if you feel very confident, add a turn-based multiplayer mode where players compete to see who gets the best score.

SideShooter

This game was our last, so it has the most complex of features for use, but that doesn't mean we cannot expand it. This game can use many more weapons, enemies, and levels for the players to enjoy. We can also try the many other effects that come with Construct Classic, or the free ones on the Scirra forums.

Tips and tricks

Construct Classic is a giant program, and we would not be able to cover every feature or use that we still have to learn. But now we'll take a quick look to see some other techniques that might prove useful in our future games.

For these examples, we'll be using graphics from the following image:

Custom collision masks

Sometimes, we will need to give our objects custom collision masks rather than using the built-in collision system. Luckily, Construct Classic makes this as easy as drawing our main sprites.

Start by adding in the ground block sprites with the `Solid` attribute. Then, add a sprite with the platform behavior. Notice how the sprite collides with the outer edges of the ground blocks when it should walk along the middle of their top plane.

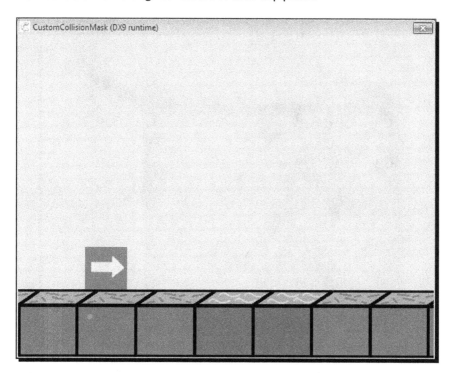

We will now edit the collision mask for the blocks manually. If you're running Construct Classic on a Windows Vista or a Windows 7 computer, be sure to run it with the **Run as administrator** option (right-click on the icon to find the option) or you will not be able to edit the files needed.

In the `Animator` properties of a block, right-click and select `Launch Explorer`. Don't click on any dialog buttons yet; switch over to the folder it opens instead. In this folder, each frame of the animation will have a `Frame` and `Mask` image respectively.

Unfortunately, the built-in paint program for Windows does not support transparency, so we will need to edit the `Mask 1.png` file in a more advanced tool such as Photoshop, or its free alternative **Paint.NET**. Load up the image and then edit it to match the following image before saving it:

Collision masks will make objects collide wherever there are non-transparent pixels, so when we return to Construct Classic, answer **Ok** and **Yes** to the two dialog boxes that appear. If Construct Classic leaves the files behind, they can be deleted but will be overwritten anyway when you edit an animation this way.

Do this to the water sprite as well, and then run the game to see what our result is.

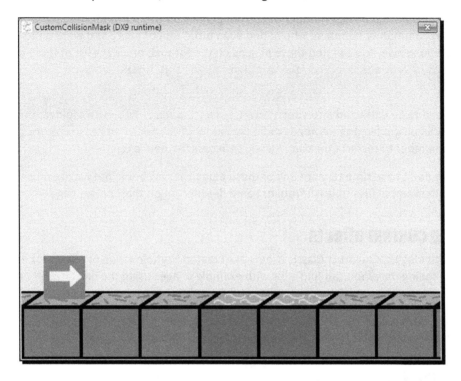

By using custom collision masks, we were able to save the usage of an invisible sprite or box object to replicate the effect seen in the previous image. Such tricks improve the efficiency of any games we make, and hence we should use it whenever the alternative requires adding many more objects.

Adding custom plugins

Construct Classic has a large number of custom plugins on the Scirra forums. These are posted by community members who added even more functionality and went on to share it with everyone else. You can find these plugins on the forums, or view a list of them using the link `http://www.scirra.com/forum/list-of-all-plugins-add-on_topic44307.html`.

These need to be extracted into your `\Construct Classic\Plugins\` folder. If the file is a single CSX plugin file, then it needs to be copied to `\Construct Classic\Runtime\` as well. Remember to restart Construct Classic to access the new plugins.

Sadly, we don't have time to learn any of these plugins in this book, but luckily, most of them come with example files to learn from or some description on their plugin page.

Adding custom effects

Along with plugins, Construct Classic users have created a whole range of effects for everyone to use in their games. You can find a list with example images using the link `http://www.scirra.com/forum/list-of-all-effects-add-on_topic44302.html`.

These are extracted to the `\Construct Classic\Effects\` folder. Construct Classic will need to be restarted if it is open for the new effects to appear.

Using the Canvas object

The **Canvas** object is able to draw shapes or copy sprite images into it and then update its collision mask to suit this. This makes them great for making destructible terrain, or even a painting program.

Start a blank project, add a Canvas object, and stretch it to fit the whole layout. Next, insert the `Pencil` image as a `Sprite`. Give this a `hotspot` in the bottom-left corner (*numpad 1*) and behavior `Mouse`. Add the `Mouse & Keyboard` object before going into the **Event Sheet Editor**.

Add an event for the `Start of layout`, and for the `MouseKeyboard` object add the action `Set cursor visible` to set the mouse cursor to `Invisible`.

Create an event for when the `Left mouse button is down` and have the `Canvas` object action `Draw point` to draw at `Pencil.X` and `Pencil.Y`. Note that the `Canvas` object has many other drawing commands that could be used such as drawing lines, a filled rectangle, or even pasting a sprite into itself.

Following this, add an event for `On Right mouse Clicked` and give it the `Clear to transparent` action for the `Canvas` object. We now have a basic paint program!

If we wanted objects to collide with the `Canvas` object, then we'd need to run the `Update collision mask` action whenever we change the image.

The `Canvas` object does have one limitation: it does not work as efficiently with scrolling layouts as it does with non-scrolling layouts. Although a work-around can be found to minimize limitations such as this, it is best to find another method of terrain destruction for big layouts.

Using the Minimap object

The **Minimap** object makes radar much easier by automatically plotting points or even sprites as terrain.

We'll start by creating a blank project and creating two different sprites: one to represent enemies and the other to represent the player. Give the player object the `8 Direction` behavior and the `Center view on me` attribute before setting the layout to having `Unbounded scrolling` ticked in its properties.

Place many enemy sprites around the player, and then create a stationary (0% scroll rates) `HUD` layer with the `Minimap` object inserted into the top-right corner of the layout. Set the `Points size` setting of the `Minimap` object to `3` and go to the **Event Sheet Editor**.

Add an `Always` event and give it the `Minimap` action `Plot object` for the player and enemy objects. Choose a color for each object, and then run the game to see the `Minimap` in action.

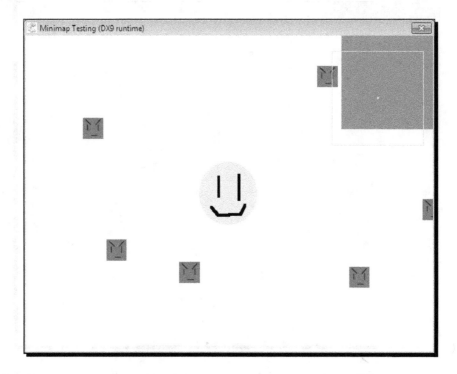

The Minimap has been helping players navigate their way through levels for over a decade, so it's always good to know how to make them.

Using the Plasma object

The **Plasma** object can be used to create trails without processor-intensive pixel shader effects.

Create a new project and place a `Plasma` object stretched across the layout, before creating a sprite with the skull graphic and the behavior `Mouse`.

In the **Event Sheet Editor**, add an `Always` event and give it the `Plasma` action `Paste object` to paste `Skull` into it. Run the application to see our effect in action.

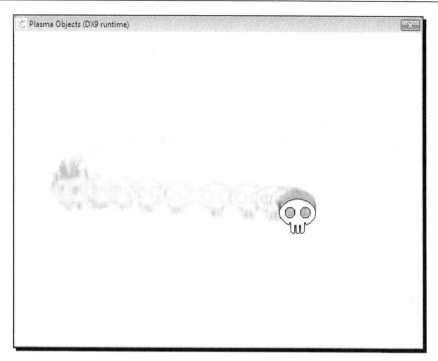

Note how the trail runs at full speed and that the `Plasma` object has properties that can adjust its settings and behavior, which means it can be used for many more effect types than a trail fade. Similar to the `Minimap` object, `Plasma` objects do not do well with scrolling layouts and so should be on a layer that does not scroll.

Make backups often; make saves even more

The best tip for Construct Classic is to save often and to keep backups. Construct Classic can perform these itself by changing settings in the **File** | **Preferences** menu. Set `Auto Saves` and `Auto backup saves` to `true` in order to keep your work safe.

As Construct Classic is constantly in development, sometimes bugs may occur that require you to go back to an old version of your program. So it's good to take manual backups as well.

Finding help

Sadly, there are so many objects and features of Construct Classic that we can't cover the usage of every one of them, but that's where the Construct communities come to the rescue.

Whenever you get stuck, there is help available online for most problems you might encounter and communities of people willing to help you out. Construct Classic has many user groups from different backgrounds in the game development. Any problems you might have can be addressed online with the tutorials and information that members share on the Scirra forums.

Try visiting the **Help & Support using Construct Classic** or **Your tutorials & example files** sub-forums of the Construct Classic forum section to see if your question has already been asked and solved, or feel free to share your issue with the forums. If you're certain that your problem is a bug, you can even submit it there, and a community member will try to fix it for a later release of Construct Classic.

A note on Construct 2

This book focuses on Construct Classic, but Construct 2 existed at the time of its writing. It's worth knowing that our games cannot be ported over to Construct 2, as they work on different engines (Construct Classic is DirectX-based, while Construct 2 exports to HTML5 and WebGL).

However, the knowledge we've gained will help very much if you ever migrate to Construct 2, as it has a similar interface and event editor and will be much quicker to learn with a foundation in Construct Classic.

Should you ever need extra help with migrating to Construct 2, there is also an included manual that documents all of the features of Construct 2. This manual can also be read online at the Scirra homepage.

Summary

In this chapter, we looked back on our games and the skills we've learned while making them, but we also looked ahead by learning a few objects we might use in future games.

More specifically, we covered:

- Taking a recap of everything we learned in the previous chapters and how they affected our games developments
- Looking at aspects we can improve on in our previous games in order to make fully-featured titles
- Learning some additional skills that will help in our future games

Now that we've completed this beginner's guide, we're ready to start making our own ideas into fully-fledged games, which is where the real fun starts.

Good luck with your future endeavors, and I hope you enjoy your time with Construct Classic!

Pop Quiz Answers

Chapter 3: Adding the Challenge

Recap

Question Number	Answer
1	b. The only action that controls the entire `Platform` behavior.
2	a. The behaviors attempt to set animations to their tagged animations by default, but can be overridden by events.
3	c. We added events to have the enemies move in the opposite direction whenever they collide with solid walls.

Chapter 4: Making Noise

Sound and music

Question Number	Answer
1	d. All of the options are true of MOD and MP3 files.
2	c. Although option a is used to play MP3s with XAudio2, we use separate events and actions for the MOD object.
3	b. Our players only need the executable and any external resources that the game calls. We may also want to include the DirectX 9 Redistributable Web Installer, as the game will not run with old versions of DirectX 9.

Chapter 5: Practical Physics

Physical games

Question Number	Answer
1	b.
2	a.
3	c.

Chapter 6: Custom Levels

INI file recap

Question Number	Answer
1	b. INI files use text and number data to store information such as paths to graphics or position values.
2	a. Although it's true, only one INI can be opened per INI object at a time. A layout can have multiple instances of the INI object.
3	c. INI files can be stored securely with CRC32 encryption, but the main use of them is to provide data in an easy to read and modify format. This makes them great for custom levels, dialogs, settings, and any other data that players are allowed to modify. A simple deterrent for modifications to your files is to change their extension to a random one (such as `.zqf`). The INI object will still read them correctly.

Chapter 7: Platformer Revisited, a 2D Shooter

A shot in the dark

Question Number	Answer
1	c. The `Light` object determines a point of origin for shadows, but for an individual object to cast a shadow, it must have the `Shadow Caster` behavior.
2	b. A shadow can be any color set and will not overlap objects in layers above it.
3	a. `Bullets` are created by the `Sprite` they are to appear from and do not require an action to move along their path.

Chapter 8: I'm Throwing a Grenade!

Looking back on timers and effects

Question Number	Answer
1	b. The `Timer` behavior has no properties settings, but can be used to create multiple countdown timers for an individual object with events.
2	d. All answers are true. A game will not display the visual effects on a computer with a graphics card that cannot have a high enough and correct pixel shader model version (`Effects` in Construct Classic require a minimum version ranging from `0.0` to `2.0` in general).
3	c. Although `Effects` will generally show in the Layout Editor view, all distortions are performed in real time for every frame. This is the main reason why they can cause slow-down when many are used at once, and why they should generally be applied to an entire layer at once to reduce performance decreases.

Index

Symbols

.ext 97
.it format 95, 98
.xm format 98

A

actions 68
Add / Edit option 200
additional level
  creating 152, 153
administrator option 259
Always condition 68
Always event 136, 264
animator box 15
Animator tab 14
animation tag
  using 40
attributes
  adding, to objects 46-48
  Destroy if far 48
  Destroy on Startup 48
  Destroy out of screen 48
  No serialize 48
  Platform 48
Animator properties 259
Autoplay file action 103

B

backup
  creating 265
basic AI 238

behaviors

8 Direction 53
about 49
ball 53
bullet 53
car 25
controls setting 53
custom movement 53
grid movement 53
physics 53
players, moving 49-52
RTS 53
BounceBall, game 258
Brush tool 25
bullet shooting
  about 219
  guns, adding 219-227

C

Canvas object
  using 262, 263
Center view on me attribute 263
challenges
  bestowing 73-76
  game, ending 77
  player death 77
  player's life, removing 77
collision 72
collisions mode
  bounding box 40
  none 40
  Per Pixel 40

point 40
selecting 40
Collision Mask variable 232
Compare event 84
Construct 2 266
Construct Classic
about 5, 258
downloading 5,6
game project, creating 7
graphics, using 258
interface, navigating 11
running 5,6
using, steps 7
Construct Classic editor
basics 255
containers
using 218
Crop tool 26
custom collision masks 258
custom effects
adding 262
custom levels
Game event sheet, including 165
INI file, setting 165
loading 160-165
NextINI layout 165
custom plugins
adding 262

D

debugger
about 154
examining 154, 155
Destroy action 77
Die animation 78
Disable when
option 251
distortion effect
adding 249-251
Distort Normal effect
about 249
moving away 252
drawing tools, Construct Classic
Brush tool 25
Crop tool 26
Erasor Tool 25

Flip tool 26
Mirror tool 26
Pen Tool 25
Rectangle select tool 24
Resize Canvas tool 26
Rotate tool 26
Wand tool 25

E

Effects layer
setting up 248
Else event 140, 210
Enable python option 105
enemy
adding 78, 80-83
creating 232-237
direction rotation 84
motion direction 84
Erasor Tool 25
events
about 68
creating, in Event Sheet Editor 60-67
using 59
event editor 15
Event Sheet Editor tab 62
event sheets
about 128
creating 129, 130
ExplosionDistort object 251

F

Families 218
Flip tool 26
For loop
amount 142
Function object 188

G

game
exporting 104-109
music, adding 91
Game event 152
Game event sheet
about 243
including 165

Game Over screen
  layout, creating 166-170
game project, Construct Classic
  creating 7
  details, modifying 10
  running 10
  starting 7-10
game win
  animations, setting 72
  Set activated condition, using 72
  situations, creating 70, 71
Global property 127
Graphical User Interface. *See* **GUI**
grenade explosion
  flash, adding 247, 248
grenades
  about 241
  adding, to our game 242-246
  bouncing 246
  throwing 246
groups
  about 129
  creating 129, 130
GUI
  about 84
  background, creating 85-88
gun
  spawning 238, 239

H

Heads Up Display. *See* **HUD**
help option 266
High Level Shader Language. *See* **HLSL**
HLSL 252
Hotspot button 31
Horizontal alignment property 126
HUD 57

I

INI file
  about 157
  creating 158, 160
  groups 160
  items 160
Insert an object option 16

interface, Construct Classic
  layout editor 78
  navigating 11-14
  properties box 15
Invisible on start checkbox 23
Is playing condition 99

L

Layers tab 56
layout condition
  starting 94
Layout Editor 78
layers box 15
level editor
  about 170, 171
  Cursor object, aligning with grid 189
  edit region 188
  events, adding to 174, 176-179, 181
  events, creating for interface 181-188
  function object 188
  groups, disabling 188
  groups, enabling 188
  INI file, writing to 188
  objects, creating 171-174
  portals, placing 189
Log screen 155

M

Mask 1.png file 260
Minimap object
  using 263, 264
Mirror tool 26
module music
  adding, to game 95-98
multiplayer
  using 219
music
  about 91
  adding 148, 150-152
  adding, to game 92, 93
  looping 94
  module format range 94
  MP3 file, adding 92, 93
  MP3 file, playing 94
MyPlatformer.exe 109
MyPlatformer, game 256, 257

N

new animations
  creating 39, 40
New behavior box 49

O

objects
  about 16
  attributes, adding 46, 47
  creating 21-24
  sprite appearance, changing 27
  sprite, drawing 24-26
  sprite pictures, making 27
One-shot attribute 170
One-shot property 252
Order | To Back 85
overlapping 72

P

Paint.NET 260
parallax
  about 227
  scrolling, creating 228, 229
particle objects
  about 143
  fireworks, creating 144-147
Path Movement plugin 257
Pen Tool 25
physical force
  about 130
  creating 131-135
physical objects
  about 114
  aligning, to grid 128
  creating 114-127
  custom collision mask, creating 128
  Global property 127
  properties, setting 128
  Timer behavior 128
pixel shader 251
Pixel shader version 2 251
Plasma object
  using 264, 265

player's sprite
  creating 30-38
pop quiz answers 269-271
portals
  about 142
  ball, teleporting 142, 143

R

Real Time Strategy. *See* **RTS**
RTS 53
Rectangle select tool 24
Resize Canvas tool 26
robots
  moving away 252, 253
Rotate tool 26
Runtime Debugger screen 154
Run All button 9

S

Scirra homepage 266
Send to front action 77
shadow
  using 230-232
shadow casters
  using 230-232
Shadow Depth variable 232
Shadow filter property 230
Shadow filter variable 232
Shadow opacity variable 232
SideShooter, game 257, 258
Solid attribute 259
sound effects
  about 99
  adding 99, 100, 103
sounds
  adding 148, 150-152
special pegs
  about 136
  creating 136-142
  For loop 142
  Set timescale action 142
sprite appearance
  modifying 27
static scrolling
  in X axis 219

T

tiled backgrounds
  about 40
  creating 41-45
text boxes
  player's health, displaying 58, 59
  player's score, displaying 58, 59
Trigger once while true event 147
TurretArm object 238
two-player platformer
  about 192
  content, creating 192-195
  conveyor belt objects, creating 197-204
  game over layout, creating 217, 218
  HUD objects, creating 205-207
  level, designing 195, 196
  main game events, creating 207-216
  player character, creating 197-204

U

UziShot 220

V

variable
  global 53
  player actions, tracking 54, 55
  using 53
visual effects 252

W

Walking animation 78
Wand tool 25
Warp effect 252
Watch screen 155

X

XAudio2 object 99

Thank you for buying
Construct Game Development *Beginner's Guide*

About Packt Publishing

Packt, pronounced 'packed', published its first book "*Mastering phpMyAdmin for Effective MySQL Management*" in April 2004 and subsequently continued to specialize in publishing highly focused books on specific technologies and solutions.

Our books and publications share the experiences of your fellow IT professionals in adapting and customizing today's systems, applications, and frameworks. Our solution based books give you the knowledge and power to customize the software and technologies you're using to get the job done. Packt books are more specific and less general than the IT books you have seen in the past. Our unique business model allows us to bring you more focused information, giving you more of what you need to know, and less of what you don't.

Packt is a modern, yet unique publishing company, which focuses on producing quality, cutting-edge books for communities of developers, administrators, and newbies alike. For more information, please visit our website: www.packtpub.com.

About Packt Open Source

In 2010, Packt launched two new brands, Packt Open Source and Packt Enterprise, in order to continue its focus on specialization. This book is part of the Packt Open Source brand, home to books published on software built around Open Source licences, and offering information to anybody from advanced developers to budding web designers. The Open Source brand also runs Packt's Open Source Royalty Scheme, by which Packt gives a royalty to each Open Source project about whose software a book is sold.

Writing for Packt

We welcome all inquiries from people who are interested in authoring. Book proposals should be sent to author@packtpub.com. If your book idea is still at an early stage and you would like to discuss it first before writing a formal book proposal, contact us; one of our commissioning editors will get in touch with you.

We're not just looking for published authors; if you have strong technical skills but no writing experience, our experienced editors can help you develop a writing career, or simply get some additional reward for your expertise.

Unity 3.x Game Development Essentials

ISBN: 978-1-84969-144-4   Paperback: 488 pages

Build fully functional, professional 3D games with realistic environments, sound, dynamic effects, and more!

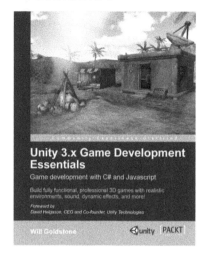

1. Kick start your game development, and build ready-to-play 3D games with ease.

2. Understand key concepts in game design including scripting, physics, instantiation, particle effects, and more.

3. Test & optimize your game to perfection with essential tips-and-tricks.

4. Written in clear, plain English, this book takes you from a simple prototype through to a complete 3D game with concepts you'll reuse throughout your new career as a game developer.

XNA 4.0 Game Development by Example: *Beginner's Guide*

ISBN: 978-1-84969-066-9   Paperback: 428 pages

Create exciting games with Microsoft XNA 4.0

1. Dive headfirst into game creation with XNA

2. Four different styles of games comprising a puzzler, a space shooter, a multi-axis shoot 'em up, and a jump-and-run platformer

3. Games that gradually increase in complexity to cover a wide variety of game development techniques

4. Focuses entirely on developing games with the free version of XNA

Please check **www.PacktPub.com** for information on our titles